T0183711

Communications
in Computer and Information Science   1089

Commenced Publication in 2007
Founding and Former Series Editors:
Phoebe Chen, Alfredo Cuzzocrea, Xiaoyong Du, Orhun Kara, Ting Liu,
Krishna M. Sivalingam, Dominik Ślęzak, Takashi Washio, and Xiaokang Yang

Editorial Board Members

More information about this series at http://www.springer.com/series/7899

Mario Vento · Gennaro Percannella et al. (Eds.)

Computer Analysis of Images and Patterns

CAIP 2019 International Workshops, ViMaBi and DL-UAV
Salerno, Italy, September 6, 2019
Proceedings

Editors
Mario Vento ⓘ
Department of Computer and Electrical
Engineering and Applied Mathematics
University of Salerno
Salerno, Italy

Gennaro Percannella ⓘ
Department of Computer and Electrical
Engineering and Applied Mathematics
University of Salerno
Salerno, Italy

Workshop Editors *see next page*

ISSN 1865-0929   ISSN 1865-0937 (electronic)
Communications in Computer and Information Science
ISBN 978-3-030-29929-3   ISBN 978-3-030-29930-9 (eBook)
https://doi.org/10.1007/978-3-030-29930-9

This Springer imprint is published by the registered company Springer Nature Switzerland AG
The registered company address is: Gewerbestrasse 11, 6330 Cham, Switzerland

Workshop Editors

Sara Colantonio
ISTI-CNR
Pisa, Italy

Bogdan J. Matuszewski
University of Central Lancashire
Preston, UK

Manzoor Razaak
Kingston University
London, UK

Daniela Giorgi
ISTI-CNR
Pisa, Italy

Hamideh Kerdegari
Kingston University
London, UK

Workshop Chairs

Workshop on Visual Computing and Machine Learning for Biomedical Applications (ViMaBi)

Sara Colantonio   ISTI-CNR, Italy
                         sara.colantonio@isti.cnr.it
Daniela Giorgi   ISTI-CNR, Italy
                         daniela.giorgi@isti.cnr.it
Bogdan J. Matuszewski   UCLan, UK
                         bmatuszewski1@uclan.ac.uk

Workshop on Deep-Learning Based Computer Vision for UAV (DL-UAV)

Hamideh Kerdegari   The Robot Vision Team (RoViT), Kingston University,
                         UK
                         h.kerdegari@kingston.ac.uk
Manzoor Razaak   The Robot Vision Team (RoViT), Kingston University,
                         UK
                         manzoor.razaak@kingston.ac.uk

Preface

This volume contains the proceedings of the workshops included in the scientific program of the18th International Conference on Computer Analysis of Images and Patterns (CAIP 2019), which was held in Salerno, Italy, during September 6, 2019.

CAIP is a series of biennial international conferences devoted to all aspects of computer vision, image analysis and processing, pattern recognition, and related fields. Previous conferences were held in Ystad, Valletta, York, Seville, Münster, Vienna, Paris, Groningen, Warsaw, Ljubljana, Kiel, Prague, Budapest, Dresden, Leipzig, Wismar, and Berlin.

The CAIP conference itself is complemented by workshops dedicated to more specialized themes, to cross-cutting issues, and to upcoming trends and paradigms. This year four workshop proposals were submitted, and after a careful review process, which was led by the general chairs and the program chairs, two of them were accepted. The workshops took place on the day after the main conference and the program included the following workshops:

1. Deep-learning based computer vision for UAV (DL-UAV 2019)
2. Visual Computing and Machine Learning for Biomedical Applications (ViMaBi 2019)

Each workshop had an independent Program Committee, which was in charge of selecting the papers. The workshop papers received about 2,5 reviews per paper on average. The workshops together received a total of 16 submissions and 12 papers were selected to be presented at the workshops. The acceptance rate was 75%.

The success of the CAIP workshops depends on the work of many individuals and organizations. We therefore thank all workshop organizers and reviewers for the time and effort that they invested. We would also like to express our gratitude to the members of the Organizing Committee and the local staff, who helped us. Sincere thanks are due to Springer for their help in publishing the proceedings.

Lastly, we thank all participants, panelists, and keynote speakers of the CAIP workshops for their contribution to a productive meeting. It was a pleasure to organize and host the CAIP 2019 workshops in Salerno.

September 2019

Mario Vento
Gennaro Percannella

Organization

CAIP 2019 was organized by the Intelligent Machines for the recognition of Video, Images and Audio (MIVIA) Laboratory, Department of Computer and Electrical Engineering and Applied Mathematics, University of Salerno, Italy.

Executive Committees

Conference Chairs

Mario Vento	University of Salerno, Italy
Gennaro Percannella	University of Salerno, Italy

Program Chairs

Pasquale Foggia	University of Salerno, Italy
Luca Greco	University of Salerno, Italy
Pierluigi Ritrovato	University of Salerno, Italy
Nicola Strisciuglio	University of Groningen, The Netherlands

Local Organizing Committee

Vincenzo Carletti	University of Salerno, Italy
Antonio Greco	University of Salerno, Italy
Alessia Saggese	University of Salerno, Italy
Vincenzo Vigilante	University of Salerno, Italy

Web and Publicity Chair

Vincenzo Carletti	University of Salerno, Italy

Steering Committee

George Azzopardi	University of Groningen, The Netherlands
Michael Felsberg	Linköping University, Sweden
Edwin Hancock	University of York, UK
Xiaoyi Jiang	University of Münster, Germany
Reinhard Klette	Auckland University of Technology, New Zealand
Walter G. Kropatsch	Vienna University of Technology, Austria
Gennaro Percannella	University of Salerno, Italy
Nicolai Petkov	University of Groningen, The Netherlands
Pedro Real Jurado	University of Seville, Spain
Mario Vento	University of Salerno, Italy

Endorsing Institution

International Association for Pattern Recognition (IAPR)

Sponsoring Institutions

Department of Computer and Electrical Engineering and Applied Mathematics,
    University of Salerno
Springer Lecture Notes in Computer Science
Italian Association for Computer Vision, Pattern Recognition and Machine Learning
    (CVPL)

Sponsoring Companies

A.I. Tech srl
SAST Gmbh
AI4Health srl
Gesan srl
Hanwha Techwin Europe Ltd
Nexsoft SpA

Contents

Workshop on Deep-Learning Based Computer Vision for UAV (DL-UAV)

Workshop on Visual Computing and Machine Learning for Biomedical Applications (ViMaBi)

Workshop on Visual Computing and Machine Learning for Biomedical Applications (ViMaBi)

Workshop Description

These proceedings contain the contributions presented at the first Workshop on Visual Computing and Machine Learning for Biomedical Applications (ViMaBi), held in Salerno, Italy, on September 6, 2019, as a co-event of the 18th International Conference on Computer Analysis of Images and Patterns (CAIP 2019).

ViMaBi was intended for researches and clinical practitioners interested in biomedical image computing and machine learning. In recent years, there have been significant developments in computational image techniques for biomedical applications. These have been mainly driven by the proliferation of data-driven methods, spearheaded by deep learning methodologies. With a gradual acceptance of these methods in clinical practice, we are at a precipice of possibly very significant changes to the way medical care is delivered, with intelligent machines being more and more involved in the process. Therefore, the aim of the workshop was to present recent developments in this fast-paced field, and to be a meeting place for academic researchers and practitioners.

The proceedings include 7 research papers, which were selected among the 9 submitted (acceptance rate: 77%) according to the recommendations of an international Program Committee of 22 experts, including academic researchers, medical doctors, and members from industry, plus 2 external reviewers. Each paper was sent for peer review to three reviewers.

The papers cover image segmentation for blood vessels (Wargnier-Dauchelle et al.) and gland (Wang et al.); breast density classification (Lizzi et al.) and microcalcification detection (Savelli et al.) in mammograms; analysis of neuroimaging data for autism spectrum disorder classification (Brahim et al.); and radiomics for brain tumor analysis in paediatric population (Talamonti et al.) and for prostate cancer analysis (Germanese et al.).

The workshop program was completed by a keynote talk by Pietro Liò, Full Professor of Computational Biology at the University of Cambridge, and a keynote talk by MD Maria Aurora Morales (Institute of Clinical Physiology, National Research Council of Italy), who offered a medical perspective on visual computing and machine learning.

The workshop chairs are grateful to all the reviewers for ensuring a high-quality program despite the tight schedule. Special thanks are also due to the CAIP organizers for their constant and timely support.

Finally, we hope that this workshop proved useful to all the participants, and set the ground for long-term interaction and collaboration towards the identification of challenges and research directions on visual computing and machine learning for biomedical applications.

September 2019

Sara Colantonio
Daniela Giorgi
Bogdan Matuszewski

Organization

Chairs

Sara Colantonio	ISTI-CNR, Italy
Daniela Giorgi	ISTI-CNR, Italy
Bogdan Matuszewski	University of Central Lancashire, UK

Program Committee

Francesco Banterle	ISTI-CNR, Italy
Andrea Barucci	IFAC-CNR, Italy
Giuseppe Coppini	IFC-CNR, Italy
Roberto Carpi	USL Toscana Centro-Florence, Italy
Stefano Diciotti	University of Bologna, Italy
Francisco Escolano	University of Alicante, Spain
Massimo Ferri	University of Bologna, Italy
Danila Germanese	ISTI-CNR, Italy
Meritxell Gimeno Garcia	Draco Systems, Spain
Li Guo	University of Central Lancashire, UK
Ayoub Al-Hamadi	Otto-von-Guericke-University, Germany
Aymeric Histace	University of Cergy-Pontoise, France
Shah Khan	East Lancashire Hospitals NHS Trust, UK
Francesco Mazzini	Tuscany Health Cluster, Italy
Leonardo Manetti	Imaginalis, Italy
Emanuele Neri	University of Pisa, Italy
Emanuele Pagliei	Cosmed, Italy
Bartlomiej Papiez	University of Oxford, UK
M. Antonietta Pascali	ISTI-CNR, Italy
Ignazio Stanganelli	IRST IRCCS Istituto Tumori Romagna and University of Parma, Italy
Lili Tao	University of West of England, UK
Tomasz Zielinski	AGH University-Kraków, Poland

Additional Reviewers

Mattia G. Bergomi	Champalimaud Center for the Unknown, Portugal
Silvia Biasotti	IMATI-CNR, Italy

Sponsor

Tecno Sistemi di Qualitá (TSQ) Srl, Livorno, Italy

Retinal Blood Vessels Segmentation: Improving State-of-the-Art Deep Methods

Valentine Wargnier-Dauchelle$^{(\boxtimes)}$, Camille Simon-Chane, and Aymeric Histace

ETIS UMR CNRS 8051, Université Paris-Seine, Université de Cergy-Pontoise,
ENSEA, CNRS, Cergy-Pontoise, France
{valentine.wargnier,camille.simon-chane,aymeric.histace}@ensea.fr

Abstract. Retinal blood vessels segmentation is an important step for computer-aided early diagnosis of several retinal vascular diseases, in particular diabetic retinopathy. This segmentation is necessary to evaluate the state of the vascular network and to detect abnormalities (aneurysms, hemorrhages, etc). Many image processing and machine learning methods have been developed in recent years in order to achieve this segmentation. These methods are difficult to compare with one another since the evaluation conditions vary greatly. Moreover, public databases often provide multiple ground truths. In this paper, we implement a competitive state-of-the art method and evaluate it on the DRIVE (Digital Retinal Images for Vessel Extraction) public database. Based on this method, we test and present several improvements which are evaluated using a dedicated performance evaluation protocol. This protocol uses five criteria and three different evaluations in order to assess the robustness of the methods' performances.

Keywords: Retinal blood vessels segmentation · Deep learning · Convolutional neural network · U-Net · DRIVE

1   Introduction

Diabetic retinopathy is the leading cause of blindness before age 65 around the world [14]. It affects up to 80% of those who have had diabetes for over 20 years. The excess of sugar in the blood weakens the capillary walls, causing a loss in tightness and eventually the rupture and the bursting of the vessels. The retina is one of the first areas affected by the degeneration of the vascular network because of the small size of the retinal vessels. These vessels can be easily repaired using a laser but the problem must be tackled quickly since the damage is irreversible. Retinal blood vessel segmentation can provide information on the vessels' thickness and tortuosity and be used to detect abnormalities like microaneurysm. These characteristics are used to evaluate the progress of the disease and act before blindness occurs. Automatic vessel segmentation is thus a major challenge in this area and many approaches have been proposed in recent

© Springer Nature Switzerland AG 2019
M. Vento and G. Percannella (Eds.): CAIP 2019 Workshops, CCIS 1089, pp. 5–16, 2019.
https://doi.org/10.1007/978-3-030-29930-9_1

years. They can be divided into three main groups: ad-hoc, machine learning and hybrid methods.

The majority of ad-hoc methods are based on low-level image processing and mathematical morphology methods to estimate the blood vessels boundaries. For example, Hajer et al. [4] use the top hat transform with a linear structuring element, whereas Xue et al. [13] developed a method inspired by saliency detection algorithms.

Convolutional neural networks (CNN) are the most used machine learning methods. In Birgui-Sekou et al. [1,2], an encoder-decoder CNN is implemented with patches and then fine tuned with complete images. Liskowski et al. [7] add dense layers in the CNN whereas Zhou et al. [16] use the green channel to enhance the detection of thin vessels after training on grayscale image patches.

Hybrid methods combine both approaches: Ricci et al. [9] achieve the segmentation using a SVM (Support Vector Machine) with features extracted from a line detector. Hassan et al. [5] combine mathematical morphology operators such as opening, top hat transform and Gaussian filtering with machine learning using k-mean clustering. A deeper analysis and comparison of vessel segmentation methods is presented in [11].

These methods are classically evaluated for accuracy, specificity and sensitivity. Indeed, a satisfying blood vessel segmentation algorithm must detect thin vessels with few false alarms. Comparing state-of-the-art methods is not a straightforward task. First of all, these methods can be evaluated on different databases. In the case of the DRIVE database, commonly used for vessel segmentation, two ground truths are provided for the test set. Furthermore, the evaluation protocol is not always sufficiently detailed to be reproduced. Because of the segmentation variability and the numerous hyper parameters, the choice of a evaluation criteria is not trivial. The trade-off between sensitivity and specificity complicates the comparison between state-of-the-art methods since a specificity increase causes a sensitivity decrease. It is thus important to use the same evaluation protocol to correctly compare different methods.

In this paper, we evaluate several segmentation methods on the DRIVE database using the two ground truths of the test set and the leave-one-out method on the training set. This complete evaluation permits to efficiently compare the methods on several criteria. As a baseline, we use the competitive work of Birgui-Sekou which presents a 95,58% accuracy, 98,37% specificity and 76,58% sensitivity [1,2]. As all the state-of-the-art methods, the weakness of this method is the sensitivity. We propose several potential improvements that we compare to the baseline implementation.

In the following section we describe the architectures tested. In Sect. 3, we present the database and introduce our evaluation protocol. Section 4 presents the results for the four CNN architectures. The last section concludes the paper.

2 Architectures

We start by re-implementing the architecture of Birgui-Sekou et al. [1,2]. We then present several variations of this architecture to improve the vessel segmentation:

the use of the green channel instead of the grayscale images, a U-Net variation of the initial architecture and the use of a different loss function.

2.1 Baseline: Birgui-Sekou Architecture

As a baseline, we choose an encoder-decoder architecture with competitive results for the segmentation of blood vessels, proposed by Birgui-Sekou et al. [1,2].

The encoder transcribes information into another abstract representation space while the decoder builds the segmentation from the features of this representation space. It reduces the space size before re-increasing it in order to find a segmentation mask with the same size as the input image. ReLu are used after each convolution to introduce non-linearity whereas a sigmoid is used for the last layer. The output is thus confined between 0 and 1 corresponding to a vessel-presence probability.

The loss function used is a sum of the cross-entropy, which is often used for segmentation, and the L1 norm to avoid over-fitting. It is defined as:

$$loss(y, \tilde{y}) = CE(y, \tilde{y}) + \alpha ||y - \tilde{y}||_1 \qquad (1)$$

where y is the ground truth, $\tilde{y}$ is the prediction and CE is the cross-entropy. We set $\alpha = 10^{-4}$.

The model runs on grayscale images calculated as the luminance of the RGB images using the weights given by the International Telecommunication Union Recommendation (Rec.ITU-R BT.601-7).

2.2 First Proposal: Green Channel Inputs

Many morphological blood segmentation methods are computed on the green input channel to enhance the contrast between the vessels and their background [3]. We thus run the baseline model directly on the green channel of the input images to see if this also improves the performance of CNN-based methods, simplifying the use of the green channel proposed by Zhou et al. [16].

2.3 Second Proposal: U-Net Variation

U-Net is a very powerful deep CNN, mostly used for biomedical image segmentation [10]. It provides good performances on very different biomedical segmentation applications, especially for small datasets using patches, for example to segment tumors and organs [6]. U-Net architectures introduce aggregations between encoder and decoder layers, combining different scale features.

We transformed the original Birgui-Sekou et al. architecture [1,2], into a U-Net architecture by adding concatenations with past layers for each up-sampling, as shown Fig. 1. We use the same loss function as the original Birgui-Sekou et al. architecture and run it on the green channel of the images.

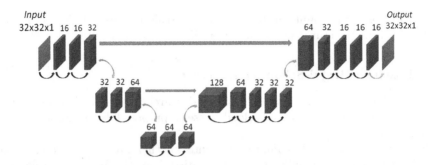

Fig. 1. Architecture 2: U-Net type. Blue arrows: Convolution 3 × 3, ReLu, stride 1. Green: Convolution 3 × 3, ReLu, stride 2. Yellow: Convolution 3 × 3, Sigmoid, stride 1. Orange: Up-Sampling 2 × 2. Purple: Concatenation. (Color figure online)

2.4   Third Proposal: Poisson Loss Function

The Poisson loss function is defined as:

$$loss(y, \tilde{y}) = \frac{1}{N} \sum (\tilde{y}[i] - y[i]) \; log(\tilde{y}[i] + \epsilon) \tag{2}$$

where y is the ground truth and $\tilde{y}$ is the prediction. This loss function greatly increases if the prediction is a false negative. As such, it seems well-suited to increase the sensitivity of the segmentation. We thus run the U-Net variation architecture with the Poisson loss function on the green channel.

3   Methodology

3.1   Database

The architectures are evaluated on the DRIVE database, which is composed of 20 RGB training images and 20 RGB test images (size 565 × 584 pixels) [12]. Each image is provided with a binary mask segmenting its field of view (FOV). The training set is provided with one ground truth per image whereas the test set provides two ground truths per image, one known as the gold standard and the other based on human perception (see Fig. 3).

3.2   Training

We pre-process these input images using the same steps as Birgui et al. [1,2]. First, the input RGB images are reduced to a single channel (grayscale or green). Then a gamma correction is applied (gamma = 1.7). Finally, we use the CLAHE (Contrast limited adaptive histogram equalization) algorithm for contrast enhancement, to make the vessels more visible.

From these images, we extract 32 × 32 size patches with an eight-pixel step. Examples of patches are presented in Fig. 2. Vessels on green channel patches seem to be more contrasted. We only keep the patches which are completely inside the FOV mask, resulting in approximately 3000 patches per image. We enlarge and balance the database by adding 1000 randomly-drawn vessel-centred patches per image. The final training database is thus composed of 80 864 patches. This database is also empirically augmented by random 90° rotations and horizontal and vertical flips.

All architectures are trained on 3 epochs with a batch size of 128. We chose the Adadelta optimizer because of its adaptive learning rate capabilities [15].

3.3 Segmentation Mask Generation

Each test image is evaluated by extracting square patches of size 32×32, with a single pixel step. Each of these patches is individually segmented by the network. The global output is the sum of each segmentation patch divided by 1024. The result is a grayscale image of the same size as the input image which corresponds to a vessel-presence probability map (Fig. 4). The division produces an edge effect which is visible on the probability maps but has no effect on the final segmentation map since the FOV does not reach the image borders.

We binarize this probability map by thresholding. A few morphological tools are then used to clean the image: smaller groups of pixels, which mainly correspond to noise, are removed and a closing is applied with a disk of radius 2 pixels in order to repair vessels. All these post-processing parameters influence the quality of the final segmentation. Indeed, a high threshold will improve the specificity whereas a lower one will improve the sensitivity. Final binary segmentation masks are illustrated Figs. 5 and 6, respectively for the Gold Standard ground truth and the Human Perception ground truth of Fig. 3. To best compare the methods, we empirically choose the parameters that result in the best compromise between sensitivity and specificity.

3.4 Performance Evaluation Protocol

Our models are evaluated on the test set with the two ground truths but also using the leave-one-out method on the training set. This enables us to take into account the variability of the manual segmentation and evaluate the robustness to the database and to the weights' initialization of our models. For the classic evaluation, the CNN is trained on all the training set images and then each image from the test set is passed to the CNN. For the leave-one-out evaluation, the CNN is trained on the full training dataset minus the current test image. The evaluation is then performed on the current test image. The resulting segmentations are evaluated using the following commonly used metrics at the pixel level: accuracy (ACC), sensitivity (SEN), specificity (SPE), Dice coefficient and area under the ROC curve (AUC).

Fig. 2. Examples of patches (size 32×32 pixels): (a) Grayscale. (b) Green channel.

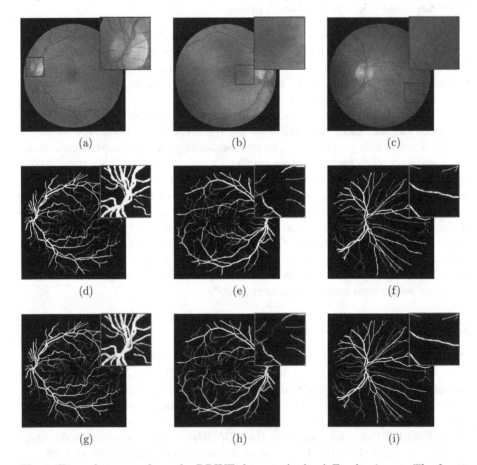

Fig. 3. Example images from the DRIVE dataset: (a, b, c) Fundus image. The fovea is the dark spot (center of image (a)), the optical disk is the light spot (on the left in image (a)). (d, e, f) Gold standard segmentation ground truth. (g, h, i) Human perception segmentation ground truth where blue represents lacks and red represents additions compared to Gold standard. (Insets) Zoom on a detail. (Color figure online)

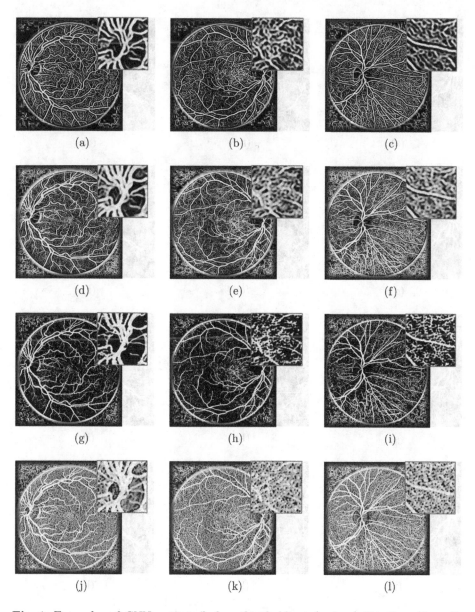

Fig. 4. Examples of CNN outputs before thresholding: (a, b, c) Baseline. (d, e, f) Baseline on green channel. (g, h, i) U-net on green channel. (j, k, l) U-Net with Poisson loss on green channel. (Insets) Zoom on a detail.

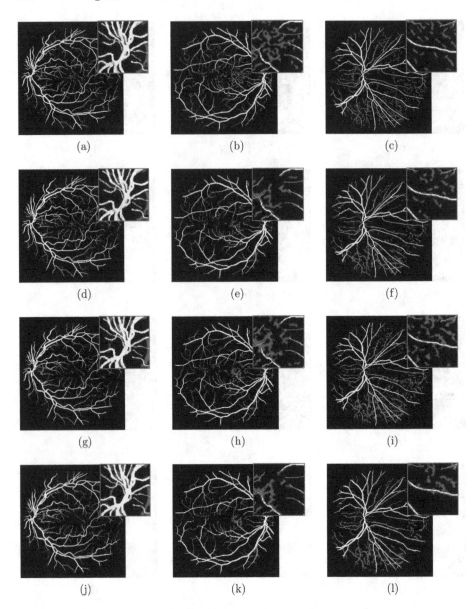

Fig. 5. Examples of segmentation results compared to the gold standard ground truth, where blue represents false negative, red represents false positive and white represents true positive: (a, b, c) Segmentation with baseline method. (d, e, f) Segmentation with baseline method on green channel images. (g, h, i) Segmentation with U-Net architecture on green channel. (j, k, l) Segmentation with U-Net architecture and Poisson loss function on green channel. (Insets) Zoom on a detail. (Color figure online)

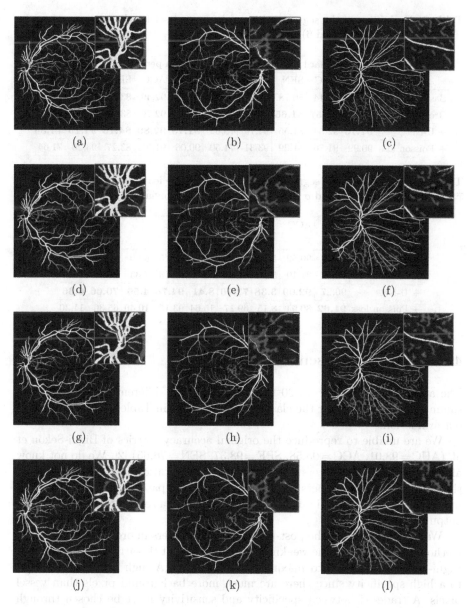

Fig. 6. Examples of segmentation results compared to the human perception ground truth, where blue represents false negative, red represents false positive and magenta represents true positive: (a, b, c) Segmentation with baseline method. (d, e, f) Segmentation with baseline method on green channel images. (g, h, i) Segmentation with U-Net architecture on green channel. (j, k, l) Segmentation with U-Net architecture and Poisson loss function on green channel. (Insets) Zoom on a detail. (Color figure online)

Table 1. Evaluation of the segmentation results on test set for the two ground truths (Example results Figs. 5 and 6).

Model	Gold standard					Human perception				
	AUC	ACC	SEN	SPE	DICE	AUC	ACC	SEN	SPE	DICE
Baseline [1,2]	90.44	92.14	80.78	93.84	72.33	90.81	92.49	83.35	93.81	73.02
Green channel	91.33	**92.57**	**81.65**	**94.20**	**73.64**	90.63	92.79	83.74	94.09	73.90
+ U-Net	**91.70**	92.54	81.55	94.19	73.62	**91.13**	**92.89**	**84.13**	**94.15**	**74.34**
+ Poisson loss	90.99	91.76	81.29	93.31	71.50	90.06	91.95	83.27	93.20	71.64

Table 2. Evaluation of the segmentation results with the leave-one-out method where $\bar{x}$ represents the average and σ represents the standard deviation.

Model	AUC	ACC		SEN		SPE		DICE	
	$\bar{x}$	$\bar{x}$	σ	$\bar{x}$	σ	$\bar{x}$	σ	$\bar{x}$	σ
Baseline [1,2]	88.79	90.82	5.13	70.41	10.18	93.75	6.90	67.09	7.40
Green channel	90.17	91.19	5.59	71.82	13.03	94.13	7.33	68.45	8.66
+ U-Net	90.27	**92.09**	**3.38**	**72.76**	**8.41**	**94.78**	**4.56**	**70.66**	**6.36**
+ Poisson loss	**91.62**	89.94	8.15	69.17	15.64	93.15	10.40	65.36	11.30

4   Results and Discussion

The average metrics over all 20 test images for the different architectures are summarized in Table 1 for the classic evaluation and in Table 2 for the leave-one out evaluation.

We are unable to reproduce the original accuracy metrics of Bigui-Sekou et al. (AUC = 98.01, ACC = 95.58, SPE = 98.37, SEN = 76.65) [2]. We do not know all their protocol parameters and thus our implementation probably varies from theirs. In the original papers the training is done on patches and refined on full images [1,2], while we train on patches and generate a segmentation using CNN output patches.

We have also chosen the post-processing parameters in order to compare the methods on sensitivity, the weakness of many state-of-the-art methods, whereas Bigui-Sekou et al. tend to maximize the accuracy. A high accuracy is linked to a high specificity since there are much more background pixels than vessel pixels. A trade-off between specificity and sensitivity must be chosen through the post-processing parameters.

The difference between the four architectures is quite small (less than 1% between the highest and lowest accuracy). However, the use of the green channel instead of the grayscale luminance improves all of the evaluation metrics, and in particular the sensitivity. This confirms the utility of using the green channel to differentiate blood-vessels from their background.

The U-Net architecture globally provides a better sensitivity/specificity trade-off: it similarly performs to the baseline on the green channel for the

Gold Standard segmentation ground truth and slightly better than this second proposal on the Human Perception ground truth. The two ground truths are introduced by Niemeijer et al. with no explanation of the chosen denominations (Gold Standard vs. Human Perception) [8]. These ground-truth dependent results highlight the high intra- and inter-variability of manual segmentation.

Using the leave-one-out method on the training dataset, the performance of the U-Net architecture is the most satisfying. This evaluation method is used to compare the models' robustness to the weights' initialization and to varying databases. The U-Net architecture on the green channel is thus the most robust architecture.

The direct CNN outputs are very different for each model (Fig. 4). The green channel tends to detect more blood vessels, improving the sensitivity. The U-Net outputs present less noise whereas the Poisson loss function drastically increases this noise. This shows that the architecture which uses the Poisson loss function learns faster than the others. As we compare the methods with the same number of learning epochs, the Poisson loss is disadvantaged.

5   Conclusion and Perspectives

In this paper, we evaluated different improvements for state-of-the-art deep learning methods for retinal blood vessels segmentation. The complete and robust proposed evaluation method permits to compare methods on many points using classical criteria. Thus, the robustness of the method to the database, to the weights' initialization and to the manual segmentation ground truth is also evaluated.

First, it shows that the green channel is a better choice on which to run the models than the grayscale lumimance. Furthermore, we demonstrate the robustness of a U-Net architecture for the segmentation task.

For comparison purposes, we used the same pre-processing on the green channel and on the input grayscale as Birgui-Sekou et al. [1,2]. The value of the gamma correction should be adapted in order to improve the segmentation performances. We also notice that the optical disk and the fovea disrupt the correct segmentation of the blood vessels. They could be detected and remove as part-of the pre-processing.

The usefulness of the Poisson loss function has not been demonstrated. However, it could be integrated in a custom loss function, with for example the cross entropy, to increase the sensitivity of a deep learning method.

Our future works will use this retinal blood vessels segmentation method for other vessels segmentation as the skin micro-circulation using rough transfer learning or fine tuning.

References

1. Birgui-Sekou, T., Hidane, M., Julien, O., Cardot, H.: Réseaux de neurones à convolution pour la segmentation de vaisseaux sanguins rétiniens - Des patchs aux images de taille réelle. In: Reconnaissance des Formes, Image, Apprentissage et Perception (RFIAP), Marne-la-Vallée, France, June 2018
2. Birgui Sekou, T., Hidane, M., Olivier, J., Cardot, H.: Retinal blood vessel segmentation using a fully convolutional network – transfer learning from patch- to image-level. In: Shi, Y., Suk, H.-I., Liu, M. (eds.) MLMI 2018. LNCS, vol. 11046, pp. 170–178. Springer, Cham (2018). https://doi.org/10.1007/978-3-030-00919-9_20
3. Dash, J., Bhoi, N.: A thresholding based technique to extract retinal blood vessels from fundus images. Future Comput. Inf. J. **2**(2), 103–109 (2017)
4. Hajer, J., Kamel, H.: Caractérisation de la rétine en vue de l'élaboration d'une méthode biométrique d'identification de personnes. In: 3rd International Conference: Sciences of Electronic, Technologies of Information and Telecomunications (SETIT), Tunisia (2005)
5. Hassan, G., El-Bendary, N., Hassanien, A.E., Fahmy, A., Snasel, V., et al.: Retinal blood vessel segmentation approach based on mathematical morphology. Procedia Comput. Sci. **65**, 612–622 (2015)
6. Li, X., Chen, H., Qi, X., Dou, Q., Fu, C.W., Heng, P.A.: H-DenseUNet: hybrid densely connected UNet for liver and tumor segmentation from CT volumes. IEEE Trans. Med. Imaging **37**(12), 2663–2674 (2018)
7. Liskowski, P., Krawiec, K.: Segmenting retinal blood vessels with deep neural networks. IEEE Trans. Med. Imaging **35**(11), 2369–2380 (2016)
8. Niemeijer, M., Staal, J., van Ginneken, B., Loog, M., Abramoff, M.D.: Comparative study of retinal vessel segmentation methods on a new publicly available database. In: Medical Imaging 2004: Image Processing, vol. 5370, pp. 648–657. International Society for Optics and Photonics (2004)
9. Ricci, E., Perfetti, R.: Retinal blood vessel segmentation using line operators and support vector classification. IEEE Trans. Med. Imaging **26**(10), 1357–1365 (2007)
10. Ronneberger, O., Fischer, P., Brox, T.: U-net: convolutional networks for biomedical image segmentation. In: Navab, N., Hornegger, J., Wells, W.M., Frangi, A.F. (eds.) MICCAI 2015. LNCS, vol. 9351, pp. 234–241. Springer, Cham (2015). https://doi.org/10.1007/978-3-319-24574-4_28
11. Srinidhi, C.L., Aparna, P., Rajan, J.: Recent advancements in retinal vessel segmentation. J. Med. Syst. **41**(4), 70 (2017)
12. Staal, J., Abramoff, M., Niemeijer, M., Viergever, M., van Ginneken, B.: Ridge based vessel segmentation in color images of the retina. IEEE Trans. Med. Imaging **23**(4), 501–509 (2004)
13. Xue, L.Y., Lin, J.W., Cao, X.R., Yu, L.: Retinal blood vessel segmentation using saliency detection model and region optimization. J. Algorithms Comput. Technol. **12**(1), 3–12 (2018)
14. Yau, J.W., et al.: Global prevalence and major risk factors of diabetic retinopathy. Diab. Care **35**(3), 556–564 (2012)
15. Zeiler, M.D.: ADADELTA: an adaptive learning rate method. arXiv preprint arXiv:1212.5701 (2012)
16. Zhou, L., Yu, Q., Xu, X., Gu, Y., Yang, J.: Improving dense conditional random field for retinal vessel segmentation by discriminative feature learning and thin-vessel enhancement. Comput. Methods Programs Biomed. **148**, 13–25 (2017)

A New Hybrid Method for Gland Segmentation in Histology Images

Liyang Wang[✉], Yu Zhou, and Bogdan J. Matuszewski

Computer Vision and Machine Learning Research Group,
School of Engineering, University of Central Lancashire, Preston, UK
{lywang, yzhou11, bmatuszewski1}@uclan.ac.uk

Abstract. Gland segmentation has become an important task in biomedical image analysis. An accurate gland segmentation could be instrumental in designing of personalised treatments, potentially leading to improved patient survival rate. Different gland instance segmentation architectures have been tested in the work reported here. A hybrid method that combines two-level classification has been described. The proposed method achieved very good image-level classification results with 100% classification accuracy on the available test data. Therefore, the overall performance of the proposed hybrid method highly depends on the results of the pixel-level classification. Diverse image features reflecting various morphological gland structures visible in histology images have been tested in order to improve the performance of the gland instance segmentation. Based on the reported experimental results, the hybrid approach, which combines two-level classification, achieved overall the best results among the tested methods.

Keywords: Gland segmentation · Two-level classification · Deep learning · Random forest

1 Introduction

Colorectal cancer is one of the most commonly diagnosed cancers, which affects both women and men. Accurate cancer grading is essential for individual cancer treatment planning and resulting patient survival rate. Different morphological structures of the gland objects can be used for grading. Therefore, accurate segmentation of gland structures in histology images is important in order to support assessment of the cancer. One of the reasons why gland segmentation is challenging is that the structure and appearance of histology images, even for the same tissue, can look significantly different. Furthermore, the gland size, shape, texture and appearance could vary significantly even within the same gland category. Due to these reasons, gland segmentation is a challenging problem. The proposed hybrid method deals with these challenges by dividing the images into tissue type categories first and solving the pixel-wise classification separately for each predefined category of the histology image.

© Springer Nature Switzerland AG 2019
M. Vento and G. Percannella (Eds.): CAIP 2019 Workshops, CCIS 1089, pp. 17–27, 2019.
https://doi.org/10.1007/978-3-030-29930-9_2

2   Related Work

A large number of published papers demonstrate that gland segmentation has become an important problem in biomedical image analysis [3–7]. This section reviews some of the approaches previously proposed for gland segmentation.

Wu [3] proposed a region growing method where featureless areas are used as initial seeds for region growing. The chain of epithelial nuclei is used for termination of the region growing. The drawback of this method is that it only achieves good performance for images displaying benign tissue, and is not effective for images showing malignant tissue, due to the deformation of morphological structures of gland objects.

Gunduz-Demir [4] introduced an approach that has employed graph connectivity to classify initial seeds for region growing. This method is different from the method proposed by Wu as it uses pixel information to represent each tissue type. The edges between different gland objects are employed as the stopping criterion. Again, this method performs well only on images representing benign tissue.

Recently, deep learning methods have been used and achieved excellent performance in gland segmentation. Kainz [5] proposed an approach, which used two convolutional networks as pixel level classifier. The input for these two networks was processed by using the red channel of original images. A total weight variation of global segmentation was used to determine the final output.

Chen [6] introduced a method based on fully convolutional network (FCN). This method takes advantage of multi-level feature representations. The network uses generic encoder-decoder architecture. The down-sampling encoder generates the multi-level features and the up-sampling decoder is used to restore the original image size and provides the gland occurrence probability maps.

Li [7] proposed an approach, which combines deep learning and handcrafted features to train the SVM classifier. Different sizes of the patches for both handcrafted and deep learning features have been tested in [7] in order to improve the performance.

3   Method

Segmentation approaches considered in this paper could be divided into segmentation with and without pre-classification. Segmentation with the pre-classification could be further divided into pre-classification at the image and feature levels. Figure 1 shows these three options adopted for the gland segmentation problem. Method 1 is a simplest approach. Both Method 2 and Method 3 use the pre-classification and are variants of the Method 1. The difference between Methods 2 and 3 is that for the Method 2 the image features are learned and extracted separately for the benign and malignant gland images, whereas for the Method 3 the features are learned for all training images and the separation between benign/malignant images is performed after features are extracted (i.e. at the feature level). Segmentation with the pre-classification is in effect a two-level classification and consists of image-level classification and pixel-level classification. The image-level classification part is to separate the histology images into benign and malignant cases, and the pixel-level classification is to perform the actual gland segmentation. The final segmentation results for method 2 and 3 are superposition of the segmentation results for benign and malignant cases.

The morphological structure of glands in benign and malignant cases is significantly different (see Fig. 3 for typical histology images showing benign and malignant tissue). To obtain good segmentation results, it is not only needed to separate the images into benign or malignant cases but also develop a way to describe the morphological structure of gland objects for these cases. In this work, two and three different target classes have been tested in order to find the best way to describe the local discriminative patterns for benign and malignant tissue. For the two-target classes, the gland and non-gland parts of the image were considered, whereas for a three-target classes case, gland inside, gland boundary, and gland outside image regions were taken into consideration.

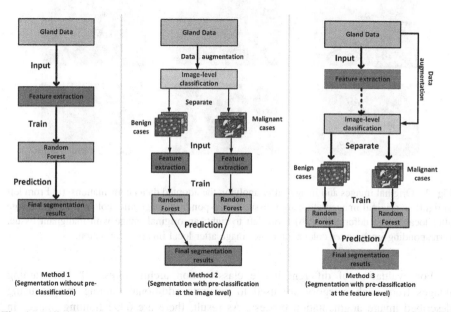

Fig. 1. Different segmentation architectures adopted for gland segmentation problem. From left to right: Method 1, represents the segmentation without pre-classification; Method 2, is segmentation with the pre-classification at the image level; and Method 3, uses segmentation with pre-classification at the feature level.

3.1 Image-Level Classification

As mentioned previously, image-level classification aims to separate the histology images into benign and malignant cases. Recently, deep learning techniques have achieved excellent performance in image classification tasks. Three different deep learning architectures, AlexNet [8], GoogleNet [9] and ResNet-50 [10] have been tested on the gland image classification problem.

There are only 85 training images and 80 test images in the gland dataset [1, 2, 18] used in the reported experiments. It is therefore important to increase the number of training images in order to avoid overfitting. Data augmentation methods, adopted to increase the number of training images use local image deformations and colour jitter.

Colour jitter changes image appearance by modifying image tones without changing morphological structure. The local image deformations are used to modify shape of structures and textures without changing the colour. In the adopted implementation, a 2D thin-plate spline [11] has been used to augment the training data. The deformation model uses fixed 10×10 grid and a random displacement of each grid point with the maximum displacement of 9 pixels. Figure 2 shows an example of original images and images after using data augmentation.

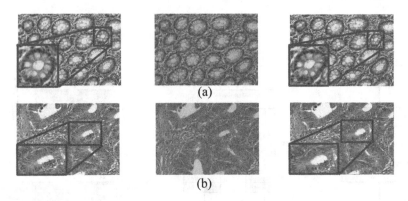

Fig. 2. Original images and images after applying the adopted data augmentations. (a) From left to right: an original image with benign tissue, corresponding image after colour jitter and image after local image deformation (b) From left to right: an original image with malignant tissue, corresponding image after colour jitter and image after local image deformation.

For evaluation of different image classification architectures, 80% of training images from each category are used to generate additional training images using described image augmentation process. As result, there are 6392 training images in total. The remaining 17 histology images are used for validation. The original 80 test images from the gland dataset are used for testing. All the tested networks employ the Adam optimisation method [12].

3.2 Pixel Level Classification

Pixel level classification deals with the gland instance segmentation. There are many types of feature extraction methods, which have been widely used in classification tasks. In gland segmentation, both handcrafted features and deep learning features have been applied. In this work number of handcrafted features were tested, including ring histograms [13], rotation-invariant local uniform patterns (LBP) [14] and circular Fourier HOG features [15], as well as deep features, including LeNet-5 and GoogleNet.

As described in Sect. 3, the pixel level classification is to solve gland segmentation for each image category. The details of two and three target classes adopted for the experiments are given below.

Two Target Classes. For images with benign or malignant tissue, the two target classes are defined as gland and non-gland (background) image areas. The labels for gland and background are provided in the gland database, with a sample ground truth shown in Fig. 3. The images and the provided two-class ground truth have been used to train feature extraction methods with the random forest used as pixel level classifier. The results are determined by using a set of morphological post-processing steps on probability maps generated by the random forest.

Three Target Classes. For images with benign or malignant tissue, the three target classes are defined as 'gland inside', 'gland boundary' and 'gland outside'. The 'gland boundary' labels are generated by applying the erosion to the original ground truth images with two labels, and subsequently performing the XOR operation between the original and the eroded images. Figure 3 shows the labels for these three target classes.

Pixel-Level Classifier. Random forest technique has been used as a pixel-level classifier to learn the local patterns in the histology images. The forest applied for the gland segmentation uses Breiman model [16]. The Gini impurity is used to split samples in each tree node. The mathematical expression of Gini impurity is given as:

$$Gini\ impurity = 1 - \sum_{i=1}^{c} P_i^2 \qquad (1)$$

where c is the total number of classes in each splitting node, and P_i is the probability of the class i.

The class output of the forest model is defined by the majority vote collected from all decision trees in the forest.

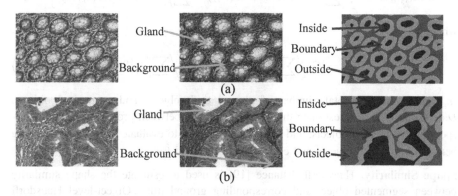

Fig. 3. Example images and corresponding labels for two and three target classes. (a) From left to right: image with benign tissue, the ground truth for two target classes and the ground truth for three target classes (b) From left to right: image with malignant tissue, the ground truth for two target classes and the ground truth for three target classes.

4 Evaluation

The performance of segmentation results was evaluated by using four evaluation measures [18, 20]: (1) detection accuracy of individual glands; (2) object-level segmentation accuracy; (3) object-level shape similarity using Hausdorff distance, and (4) object-level shape similarity using Boundary Jaccard index.

Detection Accuracy. F1 score has been used in this work in order to estimate the detection accuracy for individual glands [18]. If a segmented gland object overlaps at least 50% with the corresponding ground truth it is treated as true positive (**TP**); otherwise, it treated as false positive (**FP**). The difference between the number of ground truth and the number of true positive has been treated as the number of false negative (**FN**). The F1 score is defined as:

$$F1 = \frac{2 \cdot Precision \cdot Recall}{Precision + Recall} \tag{2}$$

where

$$Precision = \frac{TP}{TP + FP}, \quad Recall = \frac{TP}{TP + FN} \tag{3}$$

Segmentation Accuracy. Dice index [17] is a metric to measure similarity between two sets. The range of Dice index is between 0 and 1, where the higher the value, the better the segmentation result. However, in this work, object-level Dice index has been used to evaluate the Dice index for individual glands. The definition of object-level Dice index is as follows [18]:

$$Dice_{obj}(g,s) = \frac{1}{2} \left[\sum\nolimits_{i=1}^{n_g} \omega_i Dice(G_i, S_*(G_i)) + \sum\nolimits_{j=1}^{n_s} \widetilde{\omega}_j Dice(G_*(S_j), S_j) \right] \tag{4}$$

where

$$\omega_i = |G_i| \Big/ \sum\nolimits_{p=1}^{n_g} |G_p|, \quad \widetilde{\omega}_j = |S_j| \Big/ \sum\nolimits_{p=1}^{n_s} |S_p| \tag{5}$$

n_g and n_s are the total number of ground truth objects and segmented objects. $Dice(G_i, S_*(G_i))$ is to estimate the overlapping area between ground truth and corresponding segmented objects, and $Dice(G_*(S_j), S_j)$ is to evaluate the overlapping area between segmented objects and corresponding ground truth.

Shape Similarity. Hausdorff distance [19] is used to estimate the shape similarity between segmented object and corresponding ground truth. Object-level Hausdorff distance is to measure the shape similarity of individual gland objects for gland instance segmentation, and it is defined as [18]:

$$\mathbf{H}_{\mathrm{obj}}(g,s) = \frac{1}{2}\left[\sum_{i=1}^{n_g}\omega_i\mathbf{H}(G_i,S_*(G_i)) + \sum_{j=1}^{n_s}\tilde{\omega}_j\mathbf{H}\big(G_*(S_j),S_j\big)\right] \qquad (6)$$

Boundary Jaccard index [20] is another measure used to estimate the similarity between contours. It is sensitive to the infra-segmentation and over-segmentation, but contrary to the Hausdorff distance, this measure is not sensitive to boundary outliers and its value is bounded between 0 and 1. Object-level boundary Jaccard index is to evaluate boundary Jaccard index for individual glands, and is defined as:

$$\mathbf{BJ}_{\mathrm{obj}}(g,s) = \frac{1}{2}\left[\sum_{i=1}^{n_g}\omega_i\mathbf{BJ}(G_i,S_*(G_i)) + \sum_{j=1}^{n_s}\tilde{\omega}_j\mathbf{BJ}\big(G_*(S_j),S_j\big)\right] \qquad (7)$$

where

$$BJ = \frac{TP}{TP+FP+FN} \qquad (8)$$

The first term measure Boundary Jaccard index between the ground truth and corresponding segmented results, and the second term measures Boundary Jaccard index between the segmentation objects and corresponding ground truth. *BJ* is the Boundary Jaccard index, see [20] for details.

5 Results

5.1 Results for Image-Level Classification

The results of image-level classification problem are shown in Table 1. **TP** refers to identifying correctly images with benign tissue, **FP** refers to images with malignant tissue predicted as benign tissue; **FN** refers to images with benign tissue predicted as malignant tissue, and **TN** refers to correctly identifying images showing malignant tissue.

Table 1. Results for image-level classification using three different networks on test images

Network name	TP	FP	FN	TN
AlexNet	23	14	13	30
GoogleNet	34	3	8	35
ResNet-50	37	0	0	43

Image-level classification results show that the more up-to-date deep learning techniques are better in separating images in the gland dataset. Using the proposed data augmentation methods, the ResNet-50 performed with 100% classification accuracy on the available test data.

5.2   Results for Pixel-Level Classification

Tables 2, 3 and 4 show the quantitative results for pixel level classification using three different segmentation architectures for benign and malignant cases as well as the overall results. The number in bold in each column in Tables 2, 3 and 4 presents the best results using a corresponding evaluation measure. The best overall performance is achieved using Method 3 with two target classes. For the benign case, the best results were obtained with the LeNet-5 deep feature, whereas for the malignant and overall results the GoogleNet deep features turned out to perform the best.

Table 2. Segmentation results for benign cases with the LeNet-5 deep features

Method name	Number of target classes	F1 score	Object-level Dice index	Object-level Hausdorff distance	Object-level Boundary Jaccard index
Method 1	2	0.63	0.68	194.16	0.69
Method 2	2	0.55	0.64	126.34	0.66
Method 3	2	0.62	0.70	**105.67**	0.72
Method 2	3	**0.74**	**0.77**	108.18	**0.78**
Method 3	3	0.70	0.70	128.95	0.72

Table 3. Segmentation results for malignant cases with the GoogleNet deep features

Method name	Number of target classes	F1 score	Object-level Dice index	Object-level Hausdorff distance	Object-level Boundary Jaccard index
Method 1	2	0.64	0.67	210.65	0.68
Method 2	2	0.60	0.62	215.46	0.64
Method 3	2	**0.61**	**0.70**	**164.69**	**0.71**
Method 2	3	0.57	0.56	254.08	0.57
Method 3	3	0.52	0.53	230.68	0.55

Table 4. Overall segmentation results with the GoogleNet features

Method name	Number of target classes	F1 score	Object-level Dice index	Object-level Hausdorff distance	Object-level Boundary Jaccard index
Method 1	2	0.67	0.70	150.38	0.71
Method 2	2	0.63	0.65	173.76	0.67
Method 3	2	0.66	**0.73**	**136.49**	**0.75**
Method 2	3	**0.68**	0.69	202.48	0.70
Method 3	3	0.61	0.67	215.57	0.68

For the benign tissue, three-target class model provides better performance than using two-target classes. This is because the morphological structure of benign tissue is better described by a three-class target model. However, the morphological structure of malignant tissue, it is better represented by two-target class model. Figure 4 shows a sample of qualitative segmentation results for pixel-level classification. From visual inspection, the segmentation results for benign cases are better than those for malignant cases.

5.3 Methods Comparison

As already mentioned in the related work section, a number of different segmentation techniques have been proposed for gland segmentation. For example, segmentation results reported for the fully convolutional neural networks are particularly impressive [6, 21, 22]. However, interpretation and understanding of these state of the art results is somewhat difficult. Although the overall performance of these networks is very good it is not easy to associate this with any particular characteristics of the images or indeed specific parts of the network. The work reported in this paper has been focused on using random forests, as these techniques facilitate: a simple approach for using different features, changes in number of target classes, and adjustment of the classifier to work in a semi-supervised fashion to ease the burden for manual segmentation when much large datasets are available. Furthermore, operation of the classifier could be better understood, by using standard random forest analysis techniques, e.g. to find the important features, describe features interactions, or indeed relate specific features to the quality of the segmentation results.

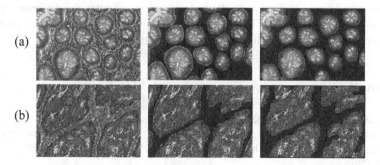

Fig. 4. A sample of the segmentation results using Method 3 with 2 target classes. (a) From left to right: test image showing benign tissue, the ground truth (gland part is highlighted) and the segmentation result. (b) From left to right: test image showing malignant tissue, ground truth and segmentation result.

Random forest have been used for gland segmentation before. A recent work on applying random forest for gland segmentation has been reported in [23]. Table 5 provides the quantitative comparison between results reported in [23] and the results of reported in this paper (Method 3). It is evident that the proposed method achieves a better segmentation performance.

Table 5. Comparison results for the methods using random forest

Method name	F1 score		Object-level Dice index		Object-level Hausdorff distance	
	A	B	A	B	A	B
Proposed method	**0.66**	**0.68**	**0.75**	**0.68**	**107**	**223**
Method using random forest [23]	0.54	0.52	0.65	0.57	126	262

6 Conclusion

The paper describes three methods developed for gland segmentation in histology images. The proposed methods have been assessed using number of different metrics evaluating detection accuracy as well as region and contour segmentation accuracy. Two of the proposed methods use image pre-classification assigning each image to two possible categories: benign and malignant. The adopted image pre-classification method together with the training data augmentation achieves 100% classification accuracy on the available test data. Overall, the best results are obtained based on using segmentation with pre-classification at the feature level. This outperforms the method with the pre-classification at the image level as the former enables more data for the feature extraction training, what is particularly important in cases of limited training data availability. Furthermore, it has been shown that the best results for segmentation of benign glands are obtained with three-class setting, whereas the malignant glands when two-class setting is used. This could be explained by noticing that for majority of malignant glands they lack a distinctive "inside" pattern.

References

1. https://warwick.ac.uk/fac/sci/dcs/research/tia/glascontest/download/. Accessed 15 June 2019
2. Sirinukunwattana, K., Snead, D.R., Rajpoot, N.M.: A stochastic polygons model for glandular structures in colon histology images. IEEE Trans. Med. Imaging **34**(11), 2366–2378 (2015)
3. Wu, H.S., Xu, R., Harpaz, N., Burstein, D., Gil, J.: Segmentation of intestinal gland images with iterative growing. J. Microsc. **220**(3), 190–204 (2005)
4. Gunduz-Demir, C., Kandemir, M., Tosun, A.B., Sokmensuer, C.: Automatic segmentation of colon glands using object-graphs. Med. Image Anal. **14**(1), 1–12 (2010)
5. Kainz, P., Pfeiffer, M., Urschler, M.: Semantic segmentation of colon glands with deep convolutional networks and total variation segmentation. arXiv preprint arXiv:1511.06919 (2015)
6. Chen, H., Qi, X., Yu, L., Heng, P.A.: DCAN: deep contour-aware networks for accurate gland segmentation. In: Proceedings of the IEEE Conference on Computer Vision and Pattern Recognition, pp. 2487–2496 (2016)
7. Li, W., Manivannan, S., Akbar, S., Zhang, J., Trucco, E., McKenna, S.J.: Gland segmentation in colon histology images using hand-crafted features and convolutional neural networks. In: 2016 IEEE 13th International Symposium on Biomedical Imaging (ISBI), pp. 1405–1408 (2016)

8. Krizhevsky, A., Sutskever, I., Hinton, G.E.: Imagenet classification with deep convolutional neural networks. In: Advances in Neural Information Processing Systems, pp. 1097–1105 (2012)

9. Szegedy, C., et al.: Going deeper with convolutions. In: Proceedings of the IEEE Conference on Computer Vision and Pattern Recognition, pp. 1–9 (2015)

10. He, K., Zhang, X., Ren, S., Sun, J.: Deep residual learning for image recognition. In: Proceedings of the IEEE Conference on Computer Vision and Pattern Recognition, pp. 770–778 (2016)

11. Bookstein, F.L.: Principal warps: Thin-plate splines and the decomposition of deformations. IEEE Trans. Pattern Anal. Mach. Intell. **11**(6), 567–585 (1989)

12. Kingma, D.P., Ba, J.: Adam: a method for stochastic optimization. arXiv preprint arXiv: 1412.6980 (2014)

13. Xiaoling, W.: A novel circular ring histogram for content-based image retrieval. In: 2009 First International Workshop on Education Technology and Computer Science, vol. 2, pp. 785–788 (2009)

14. Zhao, G., Ahonen, T., Matas, J., Pietikainen, M.: Rotation-invariant image and video description with local binary pattern features. IEEE Trans. Image Process. **21**(4), 1465–1477 (2011)

15. Skibbe, H., Reisert, M.: Circular fourier-HOG features for rotation invariant object detection in biomedical images. In: ISBI, pp. 450–453 (2012)

16. Breiman, L.: Classification and Regression Trees. Routledge, Abingdon (2017)

17. Dice, L.R.: Measures of the amount of ecologic association between species. Ecology **26**(3), 297–302 (1945)

18. Sirinukunwattana, K., et al.: Gland segmentation in colon histology images: the GlaS challenge contest. Med. Image Anal. **35**, 489–502 (2017)

19. Beachemin, M., Thomson, K.P.B., Edwards, G.: On the Hausdorff distance used for evaluation of segmentation results. Can. J. Remote Sens. **24**(1), 3–8 (1998)

20. Fernandez-Moral, E., Martins, R., Wolf, D., Rives, P.: A new metric for evaluating semantic segmentation: leveraging global and contour accuracy. In: 2018 IEEE Intelligent Vehicles Symposium (IV), pp. 1051–1056 (2018)

21. Kainz, P., Pfeiffer, M., Urschler, M: Semantic segmentation of colon glands with deep convolutional neural networks and total variation segmentation. arXiv preprint arXiv:1511. 06919 (2015)

22. Graham, S., et al.: MILD-Net: minimal information loss dilated network for gland instance segmentation in colon histology images. Med. Image Anal. **52**, 199–211 (2019)

23. AP, R., Khan, S.S., Anubhav, K., Paul, A.: Gland Segmentation in Histopathology Images Using Random Forest Guided Boundary Construction. arXiv preprint arXiv:1705.04924 (2017)

Residual Convolutional Neural Networks to Automatically Extract Significant Breast Density Features

Francesca Lizzi[1,2,4,5(✉)], Francesco Laruina[5], Piernicola Oliva[3,6], Alessandra Retico[2], and Maria Evelina Fantacci[2,5]

[1] Scuola Normale Superiore, Pisa, Italy
francesca.lizzi@sns.it
[2] National Institute for Nuclear Physics, Pisa, Italy
[3] National Institute for Nuclear Physics, Cagliari, Italy
[4] ISTI-CNR, Pisa, Italy
[5] University of Pisa, Pisa, Italy
[6] University of Sassari, Sassari, Italy

Abstract. In this paper, we present a work on breast density classification performed with deep residual neural network and we discuss the future analysis we could perform. Breast density is one of the most important breast cancer risk factor and it represents the amount of fibroglandular tissue with respect to fat tissue as seen on a mammographic exam. However, it is not easy to include it in risk models because of its variability among women and its qualitative definition. We trained a deep CNN to perform breast density classification in two ways. First, we classified mammograms using two "super-classes" that are dense and non-dense breast. Second, we trained the residual neural network to classify mammograms according to the four classes of the BI-RADS standard. We obtained very good results compared to our literature knowledge in terms of accuracy and recall. In the near future, we are going to improve the robustness of our algorithm with respect to the mammographic systems used and we want to include pathological exams too. Then we want to study and characterize the CNN-extracted features in order to identify the most significant for breast density. Finally, we want to study how to quantitatively measure the precision of the network in capturing the significative part of the images.

Keywords: Convolutional neural networks · Breast density · BI-RADS · Residual neural networks · Breast cancer

1 Introduction

Breast cancer is one of the most diagnosed and fatal cancer all over the world [8]. The strongest weapons we have against it are prevention and early diagnosis. It has been evaluated that one woman in eight is going to develop a breast

© Springer Nature Switzerland AG 2019
M. Vento and G. Percannella (Eds.): CAIP 2019 Workshops, CCIS 1089, pp. 28–35, 2019.
https://doi.org/10.1007/978-3-030-29930-9_3

cancer in her life [12,16]. It is also widely accepted that early diagnosis is one of the most powerful instrument we have in fighting this cancer [12]. Full Field Digital Mammography (FFDM) is a non-invasive high sensitive method for early stage breast cancer detection and diagnosis, and represents the reference imaging technique to explore the breast in a complete way [4]. Since mammography is a 2D x-ray imaging technique, it suffers from some intrinsic problems: (a) breast structures overlapping, (b) malignant masses absorb x-rays similarly to the benignant ones and (c) the sensitivity of the detection is lower for masses or microcalcifications clusters in denser breasts. Breast density is the amount of fibroglandular tissue with respect to fat tissue as seen on a mammographic exam [10]. A mammogram with a very high percentage of fibro-glandular tissue is less readable because dense tissue presents an x-ray absorption coefficient similar to cancer one. Furthermore, to have a sufficient sensitivity in dense breast, a higher dose has to be delivered to the subject [14]. Moreover, breast density is an intrinsic risk factor in developing cancer [13]. In order to have an early diagnosis, screening programs are performed on asymptomatic women at risk in a range between 45 and 74 years. Since a lot of healthy women are exposed to ionizing radiation, dose delivering should be carefully controlled and personalized with respect to the imaging systems, measurement conditions and breast structures. Since breast dense tissue is radio-sensitive, a personalized dosimetric index should consider breast density. For all these reasons, we built a breast density classifier based on a residual convolutional neural network. The most used breast density standard in Europe and North America is reported on the Fifth Edition of the BI-RADS Atlas (Breast Imaging-Reporting And Data System) [15]. The BI-RADS standard consists in four qualitative classes, defined by textual description and examples (Fig. 1): almost entirely fatty ("A"), scattered areas of fibroglandular density ("B"), heterogeneously dense ("C") and extremely dense ("D").

As radiologist breast density assessment suffers from a not-negligible intra and inter-observer variability [3], computer methods have been developed. One of the first is called Cumulus [1] and it is a software that works with radiologist manual input and allows to segment fibroglandular tissue. In the last years, fully automated methods have been developed in order to reduce the breast density assessment variability as much as possible [1]. In the last years, deep learning based approches have been applied to this problem. Wu et al. [17] trained a deep convolutional neural network in order to produce both BI-RADS and dense/non-dense classification. Fonseca et al. [6] used a HT-L3 Network to extract features to be fed to a Support Vector Machine. In this paper, we propose a residual convolutional neural network approach to perform BI-RADS classification.

2 Data Collection

In order to have a sufficient number of digital mammographic exams, the "Azienda Ospedaliero-Universitaria Pisana" collected 1962 mammographic exams (7848 images/single projections) from the Senology Department [11]. The dataset has been collected and classified by a radiologist, specialized in mammog-

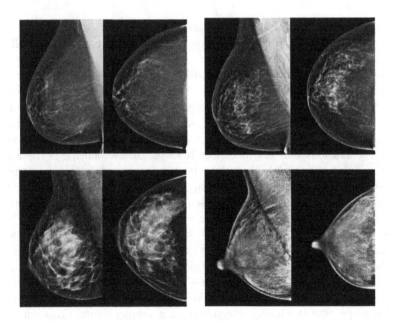

Fig. 1. Top left: almost entirely fatty breast ("A"). Top right: breast with scattered areas of fibroglandular density ("B"). Lower left: heterogeneously dense breast ("C"). Lower right: extremely dense breast ("D").

raphy, with the support of a radiology technician. The chosen selection criteria are:

- All exam reports were negative. Where possible, the later mammographic exam in medical records has been examined to verify the current health state of the woman.
- Badly exposed X-ray mammograms have not been collected.
- Only women with all the four projections usually kept in mammography (craniocaudal and medio-lateral oblique of left and right breast) have been chosen.

3   Network Model

In order to train, fit and evaluate the CNNs, Keras -a Python API- with Tensorflow in backend [2] has been used. The exams have been converted in the Portable Network Graphics (PNG) format in 8 bits, maintaining the original size. Even if the exams have been acquired in 12 bits, they had to be converted in 8 bits because Keras does not support 12 or 16 bits images. All the PNG images has been controlled one by one and automatically divided by density class and mammographic projection. We present a model based on a very deep residual convolutional neural network [7]. The architecture is the same for both two super-classes classification and BI-RADS classification. The architecture was made of 41 convolutional layers, organized in residual blocks, and it had about 2 millions learnable parameters. The input block consists of a convolutional layer, a batch normalization layer [9], a leakyReLU as activation function and a 2D-max pooling. The output of this block has been fed into a series of four blocks, each made of 3 residual modules. In Fig. 2, the architecture of one of the four block is shown.

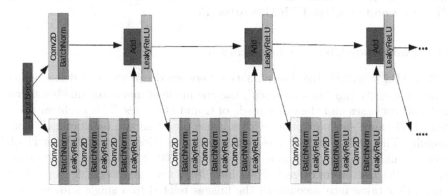

Fig. 2. One of the four blocks made of 3 residual blocks.

The input of each of the four blocks is shared by two branches: in the first, it passes through several convolutional, batch normalization, activation and max pooling layers while in the other branch it passes through a convolutional layer and a batch normalization only. The outputs of these two branches are then added together to constitute the residual block previously [7]. The sum goes through a non-linear activation function and the result passes through two identical modules. The architecture of the left branch of these last modules is the same of the first one. In the right branch, instead, no operation is performed. At the exit of the module, the two branches are summed together. At the end of the network, the output of the last block is fed to a global average pooling and to a fully-connected layer with a softmax as activation function. For both the problems, the optimizer is a Stochastic Gradient Descent (SGD), all the activation functions are leakyReLU ($\alpha = 0.2$), the loss function is a categorical cross-entropy. To evaluate the performance we computed the accuracy, the recall and the precision on the test set:

$$Accuracy = \frac{TP + TN}{TP + TN + FP + FN} \tag{1}$$

$$Precision = \frac{TP}{TP + FP} \tag{2}$$

$$Recall = \frac{TP}{TP + FN} \tag{3}$$

where TP is the number of true positive, TN the number of true negative, FP the number of false positive and FN the number of false negative. The training has been performed in mini-batches of 8 images. The CNN has been trained for 100 epochs and the reported results refer to the epoch with the best validation accuracy. In order to consider all the four projections related to a subject, four CNNs have been separately trained on a K80 Nvidia GPU. The number of samples per class in the dataset has been scaled in order to respect the distribution of classes reported on the BI-RADS Atlas [15].

3.1 Two Super-Classes Classification

In BI-RADS standard, the discrimination between dense and non-dense breast means to classify two "super-classes", the one made of mammograms belonging to A and B classes and the other made of C and D classes. This problem has a clinical relevance since a woman with a dense breast should be examined more carefully. The AOUP dataset has been randomly divided in training set (1356 exams), validation set (160 exams) and test set (160 exams). The classification scores of the last layers of each CNN have been averaged in order to produce a label that takes into account all the images related to a single subject. Furthermore, different input image sizes have been explored in order to understand whether there is a dependence of the figures of merit on the image input size. So, seven different CNNs per projection have been trained with images from 250×250 pixels to 850×850 pixels.

3.2 BI-RADS Classification

The dataset has been randomly divided in training set (1170 exams), validation set (150 exams) and test set (150 exams). Since breast density is an overall evaluation of the projections, the radiologist assigns the higher class of that subject with a density asymmetry between the left and right breast. For this reason, the classification scores have been averaged separately for right and left breast and, in case of asymmetry, the higher class has been assigned to the woman.

4   Results

We reported the results obtained for images of 650×650 pixels size in Table 1 for both the classifiers. Images of 650×650 pixel size reach the best validation accuracy but there is no evidence of remarkable accuracy trend over input image size.

In Fig. 3, we reported the confusion matrix computed for both the classifications.

Table 1. Results in percentage for 650 × 650 pixels images for both the classifiers.

Dense/Non-dense	Left (%)	Right (%)	All (%)	BI-RADS	Left (%)	Right (%)	All (%)
Accuracy	84.4	88.8	89.4	Accuracy	73.3	76.7	77.3
Recall	82.3	89.9	90.0	Recall	72.1	79.2	77.1
Precision	85.5	87.7	88.9	Precision	76.6	75.2	78.6

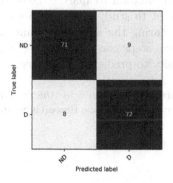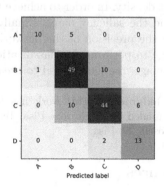

Fig. 3. Confusion matrices.

5   Discussion and Conclusions

Regarding the dense/non-dense problem, the CNN trained on 650 × 650 pixels images predicts the right label with an accuracy equal to 89.4%, which is the best test accuracy obtained in this task to our knowledge. Compared to the previous work of Wu et al. [17], the performance on the two "super-class" problem is comparable. In fact, Wu et al. reached a test accuracy equal to 86.5% with their whole dataset, which consisted in about 200000 exams. Since Wu et al. [17] studied how the accuracy changes over the number of samples in the training set, we can compare our results with theirs obtained on the 1% of their dataset. In that case they obtained a test accuracy equal to 84.9% which is lower than the one reached in this work. Regarding the BI-RADS classification, we obtained a test accuracy on 650 × 650 pixel images equal to 77.3%. This result is comparable with respect to the one achieved by previous works. Fonseca et al. [6] reached an accuracy of 76% by training their HT-L3 network on about 1000 exams. Wu et al. [17] reached an accuracy equal to 76.7%, by using their whole dataset. We are aware that a correct comparison can only be made using the same dataset. However, a validated and shared mammographic dataset is not available yet.

The test accuracy of our approach can be further increased by implementing some technological and methodological improvements. First, the current ground truth is represented by the density assessment made by one radiologist only. Since the intra-observer and inter-observer variabilities are quite high in BIRADS classification [5], we could produce a ground truth using the maximum agreement between more than one radiologist. This issue is one of the limitation of our work and we are going to collect the density assessment by other radiologists.

Furthermore, we are interested in studying how the use of this algorithm can reduce the inter-observer variability.

In the near future, we are going to improve the robustness of our algorithm including pathological exams. We want also to study weather the use of different mammographic systems influences the figures of merit. Then we want to study and characterize the CNN-extracted features in order to identify the most linked to breast density. In order to achieve this goal, we want to analyze the activation maps and the saliency maps. Finally, we want to study how to quantitatively measure the precision of the network in capturing the most important area of the image to perform the classification. These steps can help in the evaluation of new image-markers related to breast density to predict breast cancer.

Acknowledgments. This work has been partially supported by the RADIOMA Project, funded by Fondazione Pisa, Technological and Scientific Research Sector, Via Pietro Toselli 29, Pisa.

References

1. Alonzo-Proulx, O., Mawdsley, G.E., Patrie, J.T., Yaffe, M.J., Harvey, J.A.: Reliability of automated breast density measurements. Radiology **275**(2), 366–376 (2015). https://doi.org/10.1148/radiol.15141686. http://pubs.rsna.org/doi/10.1148/radiol.15141686
2. Chollet, F.: Keras Documentation. https://keras.io/
3. Ciatto, S., et al.: Categorizing breast mammographicdensity: intra- and interobserver reproducibility of BI-RADS densitycategories. Breast **14**(4), 269–275 (2005). https://doi.org/10.1016/j.breast.2004.12.004. http://linkinghub.elsevier.com/retrieve/pii/S0960977604002498
4. Dance, D.R., Christofides, S., McLean, I.D., Maidment, A.D.A., Ng, K.H.: Diagnostic Radiology Physics: A Handbook for Teachers and Students, 710 p. (2014)
5. Ekpo, E.U., Ujong, U.P., Mello-Thoms, C., McEntee, M.F.: Assessment of inter-radiologist agreement regarding mammographic breast density classification using the fifth edition of the BI-RADS atlas. Am. J. Roentgenol. **206**(5), 1119–1123 (2016). https://doi.org/10.2214/AJR.15.15049. http://www.ajronline.org/doi/10.2214/AJR.15.15049
6. Fonseca, P., Castañeda, B., Valenzuela, R., Wainer, J.: Breast density classification with convolutional neural networks. In: Beltrán-Castañón, C., Nyström, I., Famili, F. (eds.) CIARP 2016. LNCS, vol. 10125, pp. 101–108. Springer, Cham (2017). https://doi.org/10.1007/978-3-319-52277-7_13
7. He, K., Zhang, X., Ren, S., Sun, J.: Deep Residual Learning for Image Recognition. arXiv:1512.03385 [cs], December 2015
8. International Agency for Research on Cancer (2018). http://gco.iarc.fr/today/home
9. Ioffe, S., Szegedy, C.: Batch Normalization: Accelerating Deep Network Training by Reducing Internal Covariate Shift. arXiv:1502.03167, February 2015
10. Krishnan, K., et al.: Longitudinal study of mammographic density measures that predict breast cancer risk. Cancer Epidemiol. Biomark. Prev. **26**(4), 651–660 (2017). https://doi.org/10.1158/1055-9965.EPI-16-0499. http://cebp.aacrjournals.org/lookup/doi/10.1158/1055-9965.EPI-16-0499

11. Lizzi, F., et al.: Residual Convolutional Neural Networks for Breast Density Classification (2019). https://doi.org/10.5220/0007522202580263

12. Løberg, M., Lousdal, M.L., Bretthauer, M., Kalager, M.: Benefits and harms of mammography screening. Breast Cancer Res. **17**(1) (2015). https://doi.org/10.1186/s13058-015-0525-z. http://breast-cancer-research.biomedcentral.com/articles/10.1186/s13058-015-0525-z

13. McCormack, V.A.: Breast density and parenchymal patterns as markers of breast cancer risk: a meta-analysis. Cancer Epidemiol. Biomark. Prev. **15**(6), 1159–1169 (2006). https://doi.org/10.1158/1055-9965.EPI-06-0034. http://cebp.aacrjournals.org/cgi/doi/10.1158/1055-9965.EPI-06-0034

14. Miglioretti, D.L., et al.: Radiation-induced breast cancer incidence and mortality from digital mammography screening: a modeling study. Ann. Internal Med. **164**(4), 205 (2016). https://doi.org/10.7326/M15-1241. http://annals.org/article.aspx?doi=10.7326/M15-1241

15. Sickles, E., D'Orsi, C., Bassett, L., et al.: ACR BI-RADS®. Atlas, Breast Imaging Reporting and Data System (2013)

16. Siegel, R.L., Miller, K.D., Jemal, A.: Cancer statistics, 2019: Cancer Statistics, 2019. CA: A Cancer J. Clin. **69**(1), 7–34 (2019). https://doi.org/10.3322/caac.21551. http://doi.wiley.com/10.3322/caac.21551

17. Wu, N., et al.: Breast density classification with deep convolutional neural networks. arXiv:1711.03674 [cs, stat], November 2017

Combining Convolutional Neural Networks for Multi-context Microcalcification Detection in Mammograms

Benedetta Savelli[1], Claudio Marrocco[1], Alessandro Bria[1], Mario Molinara[1], and Francesco Tortorella[2(✉)]

[1] Department of Electrical and Information Engineering,
University of Cassino and L.M., Cassino, FR, Italy
{b.savelli,c.marrocco,a.bria,m.molinara}@unicas.it
[2] Department of Information and Electrical Engineering and Applied Mathematics,
University of Salerno, Fisciano, SA, Italy
ftortorella@unisa.it

Abstract. Breast cancer is the most frequent cancer among women, and also causes the greatest number of cancer-related deaths. One effective way to reduce breast-cancer related deaths is to use mammography as a screening strategy. In this framework, cluster of microcalcifications can be an important indicator of breast cancer. To help radiologists in their diagnostic operations, Computer Aided Detection systems have been proposed, which are based Deep Learning methodologies. Such solutions showed remarkable performance, but further improvements can be gained if the design of the detector takes advantage of specific knowledge on the problem.

We present an approach for the automated detection of microcalcifications in Full Field Digital Mammograms which involves an ensemble of CNN. The rationale is to employ one CNN trained on ROIs strictly containing the lesions to be detected together with other CNNS trained on ROIs centered on the same lesions, but progressively larger. In this way, shallower networks become specialized in learning local image features, whereas deeper ones are well suited to learn patterns of the contextual background tissues. Once trained, the detectors are combined together to obtain a final ensemble that can effectively detect lesions with a substantial reduction of false positives.

Experiments made on a publicly available dataset showed that our approach obtained significantly better performance with respect to the best single detector in the ensemble, so demonstrating its effectiveness.

Keywords: Ensemble of classifiers · Deep Learning · Computer-aided detection (CADe) · Mammography

© Springer Nature Switzerland AG 2019
M. Vento and G. Percannella (Eds.): CAIP 2019 Workshops, CCIS 1089, pp. 36–44, 2019.
https://doi.org/10.1007/978-3-030-29930-9_4

1   Introduction

According to World Health Organization [1], breast cancer is the most frequent cancer among women, impacting 2.1 million women each year, and also causes the greatest number of cancer-related deaths among women. In 2018, it is estimated that 627,000 women died from breast cancer – that is approximately 15% of all cancer deaths among women. One effective way to reduce breast-cancer related deaths is to use radiology imaging (particularly mammography) as a screening strategy. In this framework, cluster of microcalcifications (μCs) can be an important indicator of breast cancer [16], since they appear in 30%–50% of cases diagnosed by mammographic screenings [10]. Microcalcifications appear on mammograms (see some examples in Fig. 1.) as small granular bright spots of size between 0.1 mm and 1 mm, and they may occur alone or in clusters as a group of MCs closely distributed within a spatial region [20].

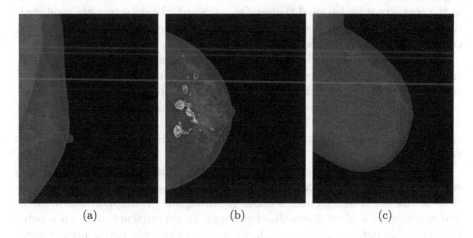

(a)   (b)   (c)

Fig. 1. Some examples of mammograms

To help radiologists in their diagnostic operations, Computer Aided Detection (CADe) systems based on machine learning technique have been proposed [2,4] in the past years, while recent CADe systems include Deep Learning methodologies [21]. Even though such solutions showed remarkable performance, further improvements can be gained if the design of the detector takes advantage of specific knowledge on the problem. As an example, methods for managing the effects of quantum noise can be beneficial even when the detection is accomplished by deep Convolutional Neural Networks (CNN) [3,13].

Another possible issue is connected to the size of the Region of Interest (ROI) on which the CNN works. Since a microcalcification is a lesion particularly small and similar to the tissue enclosing it, the detector should carefully analyze both the region strictly containing the lesion and the surrounding tissue in order to guarantee a robust recognition of the microcalcification and minimize false positives. However, a unique, fixed size for the ROI makes the CNN not completely efficient at capturing at the same time and with the same accuracy both the lesion and the surrounding context of a lesion. In fact, if the ROI is defined so as to strictly contain the lesion, it may be too small to produce a set of sufficiently discriminating representations. On the other hand, a larger ROI would include much more background which can bias the detector system and increase the false positives [12,18].

In this paper, we present an approach for the automated detection of micro-calcifications in Full Field Digital Mammograms (FFDM) which involves an ensemble of CNNs, each one specifically designed to learn a different view of the same lesion. Based on linear combination of classifiers [14], the rationale is to employ one CNN trained on ROIs strictly containing the lesions to be detected together with other CNNS trained on ROIs centered on the same lesions, but progressively larger. The depth of the networks is also increased as the size of the ROIs increases. In this way, shallower networks become specialized in learning local image features, whereas deeper ones are well suited to learn patterns of the contextual background tissues. Once trained, the detectors are combined together to obtain a final ensemble that can effectively detect lesions with a substantial reduction of false positives.

Recently, few other works have tried to add contextual information into the training phase. In [7] a two-pathway CNN architecture is proposed for brain tumour segmentation. Similarly, [9] employed a dual pathway architecture that processes 3-D input images at multiple scales simultaneously for accurate brain lesion segmentation. In the framework of μC detection, [22] proposed a context-sensitive Deep Neural Network merging, at training time, features coming from two different subnetworks.

In our approach the networks are separately trained and the probability scores are merged at inference time, by allowing to focus on more different portions of the lesion background, without requiring a high computational burden and resulting in a more discriminating power. In experiments made on a publicly available dataset, our approach obtained significantly better performance with respect to the best single detector in the ensemble, so demonstrating its effectiveness.

2   The Proposed Approach

2.1   The General Architecture

As said before, the approach we propose for μC detection is based on a CNN ensemble. In particular, the ensemble consists of K different CNNs that are aimed at managing different spatial context of the lesions and thus to specialize both on local features and on contextual ones. To this end, each network of the ensemble is trained by using image patches of different size, but centered on the same detection location.

The size of the smallest patches is chosen so as to entirely contain a single lesion. Such patches are used to train a CNN with architecture inspired by the VGG-Net model [19], containing two *banks*, each made of two convolutional layers interlaced by a ReLu activation function and followed by a max pooling layer. The convolutions employ 3×3 kernels with stride 1, while the max pooling layer has stride 2. In this way, the image patches are halved after each passage through a bank. For each of the remaining CNNs, the size of the input patches is doubled and a bank is added. In this way, if m is the size of the smallest patch (i.e. the one strictly containing the lesion) and our ensemble contains K different networks, each CNN is trained on image patches of size $s = \left\{ 2^{i-1}m \times 2^{i-1}m \right\}$ and is built with $d = i + 1$ banks, $\forall i = 1, 2, \ldots, K$.

Each of the K CNNs ends with three fully connected layers intertwined with two dropout layers. At the end, a softmax function is applied to the two-output neurons to generate a two-value probability vector associated to each prediction. The K networks are individually trained and the output values $Z_i, \forall i = 1, \ldots, K$ of the K CNNs are merged together at inference time to aggregate the multi-level contextual information for the final classification. In particular, the confidence degrees produced by the networks are averaged, resulting in a single probability vector $Z_{en} = \{Z_{en,p}, Z_{en,n}\}$ associated to each patch, stating the final decision about that sample.

The final architecture of the ensemble along with the dimension details of each CNNs are illustrated in Fig. 2.

2.2 Specializing the Architecture for μC Detection

The proposed ensemble consists of K specialized CNNs that learn different spatial context. To properly define the ensemble of networks and to take into account the right spatial information, we analysed the size distribution of the microcalcifications and the spatial resolution of the training images. We found that the minimal ROI containing a μC was 12×12 and thus we set $m = 12$. The patch dimensions were doubled up to 96×96 pixels. Larger image portions were not considered because uninformative about the context of the lesion. According to these values, the final ensemble is made up of $K = 4$ networks, the first ones more focused on learning details of the microcalcifications and the others on learning context information.

2.3 Choosing the Training Parameters

In the same way as similar CADe applications, μC detection leads to heavily unbalanced classification problems. In order to eliminate the class skew during the training stage, we applied data augmentation by randomly flipping the patches horizontally and vertically and by randomly rotating the patches 90°, 180°, and 270°. Once generated, image patches were standardized by mean subtraction and normalization to unit variance [11].

As to weight initialization and training parameters, all the CNNs of the ensemble were treated in the same way. All weights in all the layers were initialized by using Xavier method [6]. Softmax loss function was adopted with Mini-Batch Stochastic Gradient Descent. The mini-batch size was of 32 samples and in each mini-batch positive and negative samples were balanced. The learning rate was set to the initial value of 10^{-3} and decreased during training by a

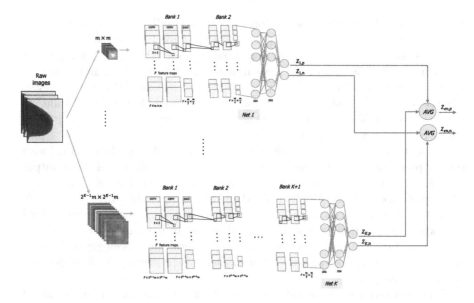

Fig. 2. Details of the proposed architecture: K is the number of the composing CNNs; m is the size of the ROI strictly containing the lesion of interest; F is the number of the chosen feature maps.

factor of 10 every 6 epochs. The learning was stopped after 30 epochs. Momentum and weight decay were set respectively to 0.9 and 5×10^{-4}. The number of feature maps was set to 32, whereas dropout was performed with a probability of 0.5.

3   Experimental Results

For assessing the performance of the proposed approach, we used the publicly available INbreast database [17], made available by the Breast Centre of the University Hospital of Porto, Portugal. The mammograms were acquired between April 2008 and July 2010 with a MammoNovation Siemens full field digital acquisition system, equipped with a solid-state detector of amorphous selenium. The images have dimensions 3328 × 4084 or 2560 × 3328 pixels, with pixel-size of 70 µm and 14-bit contrast resolution. The database contains 410 images coming from 115 cases. Several types of lesions such as masses, calcifications, and architectural distortions are included. Among the 410 images, calcifications can be found in 301 images, for a total of 6,880 individual calcifications. All mammograms are provided with ground-truth manually annotated and segmented by expert radiologists.

A large number of image patches (5,628 positive samples and 26,887,769 negative ones) were extracted from the mammograms to train the CNNs. Each patch was labeled as positive or negative according to the information provided by the ground-truth. The patches were extracted by centering the ROI on the annotated μC centers, whereas background tissue patches were extracted from the remaining regions of the images with overlapping sliding windows. Different subwindows of different size were extracted around the same center.

The whole system was implemented with a modified version of the Caffe framework [8] on a workstation with 2 Intel Xeon e5-2609, 256 GB of RAM and 2 GPU NVIDIA Titan Xp.

To evaluate the performance of the proposed ensemble, we applied an image-based 2-fold cross validation for all the experiments. In each cross validation step, each detector was trained on the 50% of the images and tested on the other 50%. When splitting the data into training and test sets, the patches belonging to the same image were assigned to the same set.

The detectors were evaluated in terms of Receiver Operating Characteristics (ROC) curve by plotting True Positive Rate (TPR) against False Positive Rate (FPR) for a series of thresholds on the detector output associated to each sample. Furthermore, the mean sensitivity of the ROC curve in the specificity range on a logarithmic scale was calculated and compared. The mean sensitivity [15] is defined as:

$$\overline{S}(a,b) = \frac{1}{ln(b) - ln(a)} \int_a^b \frac{s(f)}{f} df \tag{1}$$

where a and b are the lower and upper bound of the false positive fraction and $s(f)$ is the sensitivity at the false positive fraction f. The range $[a,b]$ in Eq. 1 was set to $\left[10^{-6}, 10^{-1}\right]$, which represents the typical specificity range of interest for μC detection [5].

For the experimental evaluation, we firstly investigated the performance of the standalone CNNs, by varying the input patch size along with the network depth. In Table 1, the performance of the individually trained CNNs for growing values of patch size and network depth are reported. We can see that using larger

Table 1. Results of mean detection sensitivity for standalone CNNs.

Network	m	d	$\overline{S}$
CNN1	12	2	76.30
CNN2	24	3	76.90
CNN3	48	4	77.45
CNN4	96	5	75.83

Table 2. Results of mean detection sensitivity for ensembles of CNNs

Ensemble	m	d	$\overline{S}$
{CNN1,CNN2}	{12,24}	{2,3}	79.51
{CNN1,CNN2,CNN3}	{12,24,48}	{2,3,4}	81.39
{CNN1,CNN2,CNN3,CNN4}	{12,24,48,96}	{2,3,4,5}	**83.54**

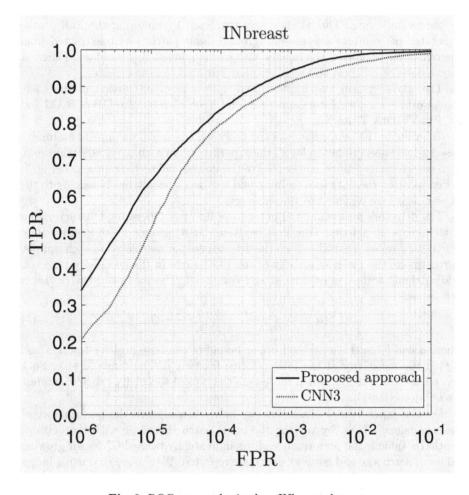

Fig. 3. ROC curves obtained on INbreast dataset.

patches (and thus including more context information) with a deeper network is beneficial to improve detection performance up to a certain size (i.e. 48×48 for CNN3). With a patch size of 96×96 the performance decreases because the representations learned are not able at capturing the lesion and the surrounding context at the same time and with the same accuracy.

In order to understand how joint predictions of the individual CNNs affects the performance, we report in Table 2 the results obtained by combining the single networks. We can see that detection performance increases each time we add a new CNN to the ensemble, obtaining the best performance measure when all the networks are used. It is worth nothing that, even when a single CNNs does not perform very well (as in the extreme cases of patch size 12 and 96) they still give a contribution when added to the ensemble.

In order to gain some more insight into the obtained results, we compared our approach and the best single CNN in terms of the ROC curve obtained on the test set. To this aim, we adopted the same specificity range assumed for evaluating the mean sensitivity. Also in this case, our approach showed notably higher performance than the best single detector (see Fig. 3)

4   Conclusions and Future Work

In this paper, we proposed an approach for the automated detection of microcalcifications in Full Field Digital Mammograms which is based on the combination of several CNNs, each one specifically designed to learn a different view of the same lesion. The rationale behind this approach was the assumption that a set of different detectors, based on different representations derived from the different contexts, can be combined in order to overcome the limitations of single-pathway networks and to improve the detection capability of each single detector. The validity of such assumption was proved by the results obtained on a publicly available dataset. This suggests to continue this work, trying to extend the proposed method to similar CADe problems as well as to explore other network architectures and combining methods.

Acknowledgment. The authors gratefully acknowledge the support of NVIDIA Corporation for the donation of the Titan Xp GPUs.

References

1. Breast cancer. Technical report, World Health Organization (2019). https://www. who.int/cancer/prevention/diagnosis-screening/breast-cancer/en/
2. Bria, A., Karssemeijer, N., Tortorella, F.: Learning from unbalanced data: a cascade-based approach for detecting clustered microcalcifications. Med. Image Anal. **18**(2), 241–252 (2014)
3. Bria, A., et al.: Improving the automated detection of calcifications using adaptive variance stabilization. IEEE Trans. Med. Imaging **37**(8), 1857–1864 (2018)
4. Bria, A., Marrocco, C., Karssemeijer, N., Molinara, M., Tortorella, F.: Deep cascade classifiers to detect clusters of microcalcifications. In: Tingberg, A., Lång, K., Timberg, P. (eds.) IWDM 2016. LNCS, vol. 9699, pp. 415–422. Springer, Cham (2016). https://doi.org/10.1007/978-3-319-41546-8_52
5. Bria, A., Marrocco, C., Molinara, M., Tortorella, F.: An effective learning strategy for cascaded object detection. Inf. Sci. **340–341**, 17–26 (2016)
6. Glorot, X., Bengio, Y.: Understanding the difficulty of training deep feedforward neural networks. In: Proceedings of the Thirteenth International Conference on Artificial Intelligence and Statistics, pp. 249–256 (2010)
7. Havaei, M., et al.: Brain tumor segmentation with deep neural networks. Med. Image Anal. **35**, 18–31 (2017)
8. Jia, Y., et al.: Caffe: convolutional architecture for fast feature embedding. In: Proceedings of the 22nd ACM International Conference on Multimedia, pp. 675–678. ACM (2014)

9. Kamnitsas, K., et al.: Efficient multi-scale 3D CNN with fully connected CRF for accurate brain lesion segmentation. Med. Image Anal. **36**, 61–78 (2017)
10. Kopans, D.B.: Breast Imaging, 3rd edn. Williams & Wilkins, Philadelphia (2007)
11. LeCun, Y.A., Bottou, L., Orr, G.B., Müller, K.-R.: Efficient BackProp. In: Montavon, G., Orr, G.B., Müller, K.-R. (eds.) Neural Networks: Tricks of the Trade. LNCS, vol. 7700, pp. 9–48. Springer, Heidelberg (2012). https://doi.org/10.1007/978-3-642-35289-8_3
12. Li, C., Zhu, G., Wu, X., Wang, Y.: False-positive reduction on lung nodules detection in chest radiographs by ensemble of convolutional neural networks. IEEE Access **6**, 16060–16067 (2018)
13. Marrocco, C., et al.: Mammogram denoising to improve the calcification detection performance of convolutional nets, vol. 10718. SPIE (2018)
14. Marrocco, C., Molinara, M., Tortorella, F.: Exploiting AUC for optimal linear combinations of dichotomizers. Pattern Recogn. Lett. **27**(8), 900–907 (2006)
15. Mordang, J.-J., Janssen, T., Bria, A., Kooi, T., Gubern-Mérida, A., Karssemeijer, N.: Automatic microcalcification detection in multi-vendor mammography using convolutional neural networks. In: Tingberg, A., Lång, K., Timberg, P. (eds.) IWDM 2016. LNCS, vol. 9699, pp. 35–42. Springer, Cham (2016). https://doi.org/10.1007/978-3-319-41546-8_5
16. Mordang, J., et al.: The importance of early detection of calcifications associated with breast cancer in screening. Breast Cancer Res. Treat. **167**(2), 451–458 (2018)
17. Moreira, I.C., Amaral, I., Domingues, I., Cardoso, A., Cardoso, M.J., Cardoso, J.S.: Inbreast: toward a full-field digital mammographic database. Acad. Radiol. **19**(2), 236–248 (2012)
18. Shi, Z., et al.: A deep CNN based transfer learning method for false positive reduction. Multimedia Tools Appl. **78**, 1–17 (2018)
19. Simonyan, K., Zisserman, A.: Very deep convolutional networks for large-scale image recognition. arXiv preprint arXiv:1409.1556 (2014)
20. Stomper, P.C., Geradts, J., Edge, S.B., Levine, E.G.: Mammographic predictors of the presence and size of invasive carcinomas associated with malignant microcalcification lesions without a mass. Am. J. Roentgenol. **181**(6), 1679–1684 (2003)
21. Trovini, G., et al.: A deep learning framework for micro-calcification detection in 2D mammography and c-view, vol. 10718. SPIE (2018)
22. Wang, J., Yang, Y.: A context-sensitive deep learning approach for microcalcification detection in mammograms. Pattern Recogn. **78**, 12–22 (2018)

Classification of Autism Spectrum Disorder Through the Graph Fourier Transform of fMRI Temporal Signals Projected on Structural Connectome

Abdelbasset Brahim[(⊠)], Mehdi Hajjam El Hassani, and Nicolas Farrugia

IMT Atlantique, Brest, France
{abdelbasset.brahim,nicolas.farrugia}@imt-atlantique.fr,
mehdi.hajjam-el-hassani@imt-atlantique.net

Abstract. Graph Fourier Transform (GFT) could be a key tool for analyzing brain signals. In this sense, we evaluate the application of Graph signal processing (GSP) for the analysis of neuroimaging data. Thus, a GSP-based approach is proposed and validated for the classification of autism spectrum disorder (ASD). More specifically, the resting state functional magnetic resonance imaging (rs-fMRI) time series of each brain subject are characterized by several statistical metrics. Then, these measures are projected on a structural graph, which is computed from a healthy brain structural connectivity of the human connectome project. Further analysis proves that the combination of the structural connectivity with the standard deviation of fMRI temporal signals can lead to more accurate supervised classification for 172 subjects from the biggest site of the Autism Brain Imaging Data Exchange (ABIDE) datasets. Moreover, the proposed approach outperforms several approaches, based on using functional connectome or complex functional network measures.

Keywords: Graph signal processing · Machine learning · Resting-state analysis · Autism disorder

1   Introduction

Functional magnetic resonance imaging (fMRI) is a noninvasive and a safe imaging technique for measuring and mapping brain activities and it is a commonly used in the field of neuroscience. However, the analysis of neuroimaging data is a major challenge due to several limitations of neuroimaging datasets, such as, high sensitivity to noise, large number of dimensions for few observations per subject, different acquisition protocols, etc [1]. Recently, there has been an increasing interest in the application of multivariate analysis and machine learning to understand complex properties of brain networks and to assist diagnosis in brain imaging data [2–4]. However, few analysis approaches take into account both the multivariate aspect and the connectivity features of the brain, such as, the structural and the functional connectivity.

© Springer Nature Switzerland AG 2019
M. Vento and G. Percannella (Eds.): CAIP 2019 Workshops, CCIS 1089, pp. 45–55, 2019.
https://doi.org/10.1007/978-3-030-29930-9_5

In this sense, Graph Signal Processing (GSP), which is an emerging sub-field of signal processing, takes into account the underlying graphical structure of multivariate data and aims to generalize the classical signal processing techniques, such as, filtering, convolution, and translation to irregular graph/network domains [5]. Thanks to spectral graph theory [6], a Fourier transform can be defined on graphs from the eigen decomposition of the graph's Laplacian operator. Thus, GSP can be used to provide a spectral representation of signals defined on a graph, through the so-called Graph Fourier Transform operator (GFT).

On the other hand, several statistical features, such as, the mean and the standard deviation (STD) of the signal could present the most discriminatory features for disease classification [7]. Thus, in this work, we evaluate a GSP-based approach for the analysis and the classification of neuroimaging data. More precisely, we assess whether the combination of a structural graph and several statistical metrics, such as, STD applied on a resting state Functional magnetic resonance imaging (rs-fMRI) dataset can lead to more accurate supervised classification for autism spectrum disorder (ASD).

Related Work: Several approaches for the classification of ASD using rs-fMRI have been proposed in the literature [3,4,8,9]. These approaches have been employed to investigate mainly patterns of functional connectivity that objectively identify ASD participants from functional brain imaging data. In [3], the authors obtained pairwise functional connectivity measurements from a lattice of 7266 regions of interest covering the gray matter for each subject. Then, a leave-one-out classifier was evaluated on these connections, which were grouped into multiple bins. An accuracy of 60% was obtained for whole brain classification. Moreover, authors in [4], investigated several pipelines that extract the most predictive biomarkers from the data by building participant-specific connectomes from functionally-defined brain areas. These connectomes are then compared across participants to learn patterns of connectivity that differentiate typical controls from ASD patients. The best pipeline lead to 67% prediction accuracy on the full Autism Brain Imaging Data Exchange (ABIDE) data. In [9], authors investigated patterns of functional connectivity that objectively identify ASD participants from functional brain imaging data using deep learning algorithms. Their results improved the state-of-the-art by achieving 70% accuracy in identification of ASD versus control patients in the ABIDE dataset. A novel metric learning method to evaluate distance between graphs that leverages the power of convolutional neural networks, while exploiting concepts from spectral graph theory to allow these operations on irregular graphs is proposed in [8]. The authors applied the proposed model to functional brain connectivity graphs from the ABIDE database. Their experimental results show that their method can learn a graph similarity metric tailored for a clinical application, improving the performance of a simple k-nn classifier by 11.9% compared to a traditional distance metric and a classification score of 62.9% was obtained for all the sites. In addition, authors in [10], introduced a new biomarker extraction pipeline for ASD that relies on the use of graph theoretical metrics of fMRI-based functional connectivity and machine learning algorithms. Their results suggest that measures of centrality provide the highest contribution to the classification power of a model for the >30 years age group, achieving an accuracy, sensitivity, and specificity of 95, 97, and 95%, respectively.

Contributions: In this paper, we propose a novel predictive modeling approach, as shown in Fig. 1, that combines GFT and several statistical metrics of rs-fMRI time series, and we test this approach to classify ASD. Firstly, the Glasser atlas is used for brain parcellation to extract the rs-fMRI time series of each subject, then, these time series are summarized by several statistical metrics such as the temporal average or STD. Secondly, the resulting statistical measures are projected on a structural graph of a healthy subject from the Human Connectome Project (HCP) dataset using GFT. Then, in order to select the most informative features for classification, a univariate feature selection is performed using an analysis of variance (ANOVA). Finally, a support vector machine (SVM) with linear kernel is used to classify the resulting features. Our approach provides a different insight from previous methods [3,4,8–10], as it does not exploit functional connectivity matrices directly from rs-fMRI, but rather relies on descriptive statistics of time series, coupled with spatial information from a given structural connectivity using GFT. We demonstrate the potential of the proposed approach to restore informative features related to ASD, as exemplified by statistically robust gains in classification metrics when compared to other feature extraction methods, including functional connectivity and graph theoretical metrics.

2   Materials and Methods

2.1   Database

The data used in this study were collected from the biggest site of Autism Brain Imaging Data Exchange (ABIDE) datasets.[1], i.e, NYU Langone Medical Center. For easily replication, this database has been preprocessed by the Configurable Pipeline for the Analysis of Connectomes (C-PAC) [11]. It involves several preprocessing techniques, such as, skull striping, slice timing correction, motion correction, global mean intensity normalization, nuisance signal regression, band-pass filtering (0.01–0.1 Hz) and registration of fMRI images to standard anatomical MNI space. The selection of the data is based on the results of quality visual inspection by three experienced clinicians who inspected for largely incomplete brain coverage, high movement peaks, ghosting and other scanner artifacts. This yielded 172 subjects out of the initial 175, consisting of 74 individuals suffering from ASD and 98 TC.

2.2   Regions of Interest and Time-Series Extraction

The proposed approach is based, firstly, on regional time series extraction from brain parcellations. In this sense, the Glasser parcellation [12] was used, which is

---

[1] See http://fcon_1000.projects.nitrc.org/indi/abide/abide_I.html for specific information.

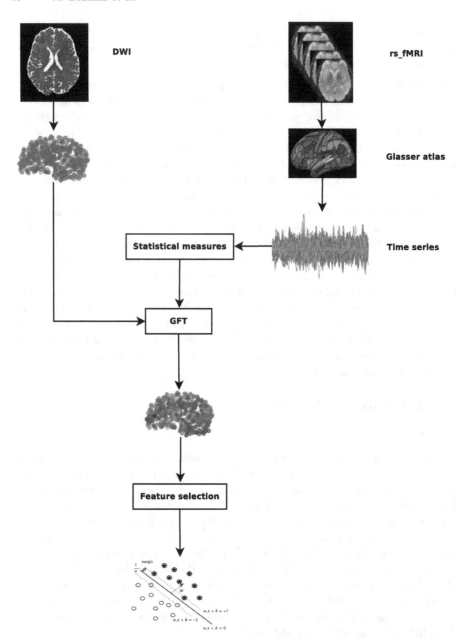

Fig. 1. The graphical framework of the proposed approach.

generated using multimodal data from the Human Connectome Project (HCP), totalizing in 360 regions. Thus, the time series of rs-fMRI brain imaging data were extracted according to 360 regions of interest (ROI) for each subject. Importantly, the same ROI are defined in the structural graph that is used to establish GFT.

2.3   Graph Signal Processing and Graph Fourier Transform on Structural Graph

In this work, we are interested in the analysis of rs-fMRI signals on a structural graph. Let us first define an undirected, connected, weighted and symmetric graph $\mathcal{G} = \{\mathcal{V}, \mathcal{E}, \mathbf{W}\}$. The graph is characterized by a finite set of vertices $\mathcal{V}$ indexed from 1 to N:

$$\mathcal{V} = \{v_1, ..., v_N\} \tag{1}$$

as well as a set of edges $\mathcal{E}$ in $\mathcal{V} \times \mathcal{V}$, and a weighted adjacency matrix $\mathbf{W}$, such that $\mathbf{W}_{ij} \in \mathbb{R}^+$ denotes the weight of the edge (v_i, v_j).

The non-normalized graph Laplacian of a graph is defined by [13,14]:

$$\mathbf{L} = \mathbf{D} - \mathbf{W} \tag{2}$$

where $\mathbf{D}$ is the diagonal matrix of degrees defined by $\forall i : \mathbf{D}_{ii} = \sum_j \mathbf{W}_{ij}$.

As $\mathbf{L}$ is symmetric and real-valued matrix, it can be factorized using its eigenvectors as:

$$\mathbf{L} = \mathbf{V} \mathbf{\Lambda} \mathbf{V}^\top \tag{3}$$

where $\mathbf{V}$ is the orthonormal matrix whose ith column is the eigenvector of $\mathbf{L}$, $\mathbf{V}^\top$ is its transposed matrix, and $\mathbf{\Lambda}$ is the diagonal matrix whose diagonal elements are the corresponding eigenvalues, such that $\mathbf{\Lambda}_{ii} = \lambda_i$ of $\mathbf{L}$.

In the context of GSP, we define signals $\mathbf{x}$ as vectors in $\mathcal{R}^N$. The spectral representation of signals defined on the graph $\mathcal{G}$ can be provided using GFT [5]:

$$\hat{\mathbf{x}} = \mathbf{V}^\top \mathbf{x} \tag{4}$$

Columns of $\mathbf{V}$ can be interpreted as Fourier modes [5] and are relevant to describing signals with respect to typical propagation modes on the graph.

In this paper, we consider a graph whose nodes corresponding to ROI of the Glasser atlas from HCP [12], with edges and weights are estimates of structural connectivity strength from a single HCP healthy subject, using white matter tractography techniques. In the following sections, we setup a supervised classification task that compare several statistical measures that are subsequently transformed using GFT.

2.4   Feature Extraction and Feature Selection

We extracted several features with and without the use of GFT, based on descriptive statistics of the temporal rs-fMRI signals. Namely, we compared the STD, variance (Var) and mean of rs-fMRI time series, Next, we computed the projection of the same features on a structural graph in the graph Fourier domain using GFT. Moreover, for comparison purposes with the state of the art, we also extracted connectivity features via the covariance estimation of the tangent matrix [15], and we use the lower triangular part of the resulting functional connectivity (FC) matrix. Functional connectivity (FC) provides an index of the level of co-activation of brain regions based on the time-series of rs-fMRI brain imaging data. Finally, we also used the FC matrix to compute three complex network measures known to be of interest in ASD research, namely eigenvector centrality (EC), node strength (NS) and clustering coefficient (CC) [10,16]. These complex-graph network modeling approaches are seldom combined with supervised learning. However, they could be relevant to identify brain sub-systems associated with ASD [16]. Thus, we obtain a total of ten feature vectors, denoted by STD, STD+GSP, Var, Var+GSP, Mean, Mean+GSP, FC, EC, NS and CC, respectively.

In order to select the best informative features and to remove non-informative features for classification, a univariate feature selection is performed by ANOVA. This technique is based on the analysis of sample's variance. Thus, the features that explain the largest proportion of the variance are retained. We tested the selection from 1 up to 360 features using this technique.

2.5 Cross-Validation, Classification and Statistical Analysis

We used the features selected by ANOVA in a supervised classification setting using a SVM classifier with a linear kernel. We estimated accuracy (Acc), sensitivity (Sen) and specificity (Spe) using a k-fold cross-validation strategy with $k = 10$. In this setting, the data is randomly partitioned into k equal sized subsamples. For each fold, this process excludes data from one subsample from the training process, and uses that subsample as the test set to evaluate the model. The cross-validation process is then repeated k times, with each of the k subsamples used exactly once as the validation data. Importantly, feature selection was also performed within this cross-validated loop.

Finally, we performed statistical evaluations and comparisons between the different feature vectors. First, we evaluate the chance level of all trained classifiers using bootstrapping by calculating a permutation test score, i.e, repeating the classification procedure after randomizing the labels. This permutation test scores provides an indication whether the trained classifier is likely predicting at chance level. Next, we compared classification metrics across three cases (STD, STD+GSP and FC) using pairwise independent t-tests.

2.6 Visualization of Cross-Validated Selected Features

We attempted to study qualitatively the stability and interpretability of the method, by visualizing feature selection with respect to cross-validation. We calculated a vector of ratios that averages the number of times each feature is selected across folds. We then visualized these ratio back on the brain using the spatial extents of the ROI. In the case of features obtained using GFT, we applied the inverse GFT to the vector of ratios before visualization. The application of inverse GFT enables the visualization of the contribution of *all* regions in the atlas, as opposed to the other features, for which only selected ROI are visualized.

Table 1. Maximum classification rates of the different approaches (max ± standard error of the mean).

Approaches	Acc (%)	Sen (%)	Spe (%)
STD	66.65 ± 0.007	63.75 ± 0.015	74.44 ± 0.010
STD+GSP	**70.36 ± 0.007**	**67.68 ± 0.011**	**75.67 ± 0.012**
Var	67.34 ± 0.007	63.39 ± 0.008	74.44 ± 0.011
Var+GSP	67.45 ± 0.006	63.57 ± 0.009	72.44 ± 0.010
Mean	62.23 ± 0.007	51.78 ± 0.015	70.33 ± 0.007
Mean+GSP	60.91 ± 0.008	59.46 ± 0.009	62.33 ± 0.008
FC	62.83 ± 0.006	56.61 ± 0.014	70.22 ± 0.015
EC	61.09 ± 0.007	57.5 ± 0.018	66.33 ± 0.010
NS	59.99 ± 0.008	61.24 ± 0.015	63.55 ± 0.012
CC	61.12 ± 0.012	58.39 ± 0.009	70.55 ± 0.011

3   Results and Discussion

Cross-validated performance of the proposed predictive modeling approach using classification metrics for the different feature vectors is shown in Table 1.

As can be seen in Table 1, classification metrics obtained using the feature vector STD+GSP, which is based on using of the temporal STD of rs-fMRI projected on a structural graph, outperforms those obtained using other statistical metrics, functional connectivity or several complex-graph functional network modeling approaches. For instance, there is a gain of 3.71% for accuracy, 1.23% for specificity and 3.93% for sensitivity when compared to STD method without projection. Moreover, there is a gain of 7.53% for accuracy, 5.45% for specificity and 11.07% for sensitivity when compared to FC method. Thus, combining the information gathered on the structural connectivity with this statistical metric could improve the classification performance. Furthermore, the classification results of the proposed method are more robust to noise than STD and FC methods, as generally indicated by higher negative log p values in a permutation test with 100 permutations, as shown in the right column of Fig. 2. In addition, Fig. 3 confirms that 100 permutations are enough to see the significance of the classification score against bootstrapped version ($p < 0.01$) for the proposed GSP-based approach.

Figure 4 depicts the visualization of selected features over folds for STD and STD+GSP with the best number of selected features for each case (respectively 150 and 100). As can be seen, many ROIs are consistently selected across folds for STD, which indicates a good reliability in feature selection. Interestingly, the reconstruction of ROI contributions using inverse GFT reveals the most discriminating patterns, as a result of recombining the selected 100 Fourier modes.

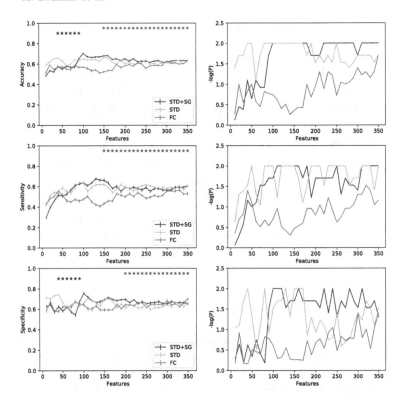

Fig. 2. Left: Accuracy, sensitivity, and specificity for the proposed method when compared to STD and FC approaches. Blue stars present a significant difference ($p < 0.01$) between the proposed approach and STD method. Red stars present a significant difference ($p < 0.01$) between the proposed approach and FC method. Right: negative log p values, indicating significance of permutation test scores with 100 permutations. (Color figure online)

Overall, the results of the present study suggest that a first-order statistical feature [7], such as the standard deviation of rs-fMRI time series extracted using Glasser parcellation could be a discriminating feature for the classification of a mental disorder like autism. In addition, projecting this statistical metric on the structural graph of a given healthy subject can help discriminate healthy subjects from patients, as indicated by classification metrics. Thus, these findings suggest that a multimodal neuroimaging approach may lead to greater accuracy than a single modality, such as functional connectome alone.

Furthermore, it is worth noting that the proposed approach is different from previous methods [3,4,8–10] in the classification of autism using rs-fMRI, in which the most popular approach is to exploit the whole functional connectivity matrix in the framework of functional connectome-based classification pipeline.

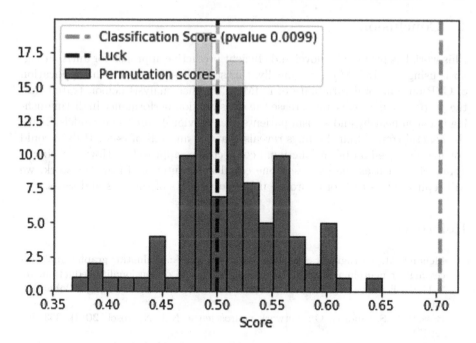

Fig. 3. Permutation scores of the STD+GSP approach and observed classification score (accuracy), using 100 permutations.

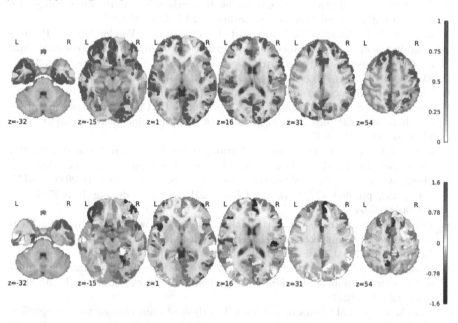

Fig. 4. Top row: Ratios (%) over 10 folds of 150 selected ROI using STD. Bottom row: Ratios (%) over 10 folds of 100 selected Fourier modes, back-projected on all ROI using inverse GFT.

4   Conclusion

This work has proposed a novel and efficient predictive approach for autism diagnosis using rs-fMRI. More specifically, this study has introduced the application of GSP on temporal variability of rs-fMRI. Further analysis demonstrated that the proposed approach can increase the classification performance in distinguishing between healthy and autism patients over previously proposed models. Thus, the general trend of our findings reveals that the analysis of rs-fMRI data could not mainly based on brain functional connectomes approaches. However, simple approaches such as the proposed one could be of interest. In further work, we will replicate this type of approach using largest sets of subjects and tasks.

References

1. Menoret, M., Farrugia, N., Pasdeloup, B., Gripon, V.: Evaluating graph signal processing for neuroimaging through classification and dimensionality reduction. In: 2017 IEEE Global Conference on Signal and Information Processing (GlobalSIP) (2017)
2. Bassett, D.S., Sporns, O.: Network neuroscience. Nat. Neurosci. **20**(3), 353–364 (2017)
3. Nielsen, J.A., et al.: Multisite functional connectivity MRI classification of autism: abide results. Front. Hum. Neurosci. **7**, 599 (2013)
4. Abraham, A., et al.: Deriving reproducible biomarkers from multi-site resting-state data: an autism-based example. NeuroImage **147**, 736–745 (2017)
5. Shuman, D.I., Narang, S.K., Frossard, P., Ortega, A., Vandergheynst, P.: The emerging field of signal processing on graphs: extending high-dimensional data analysis to networks and other irregular domains. IEEE Signal Process. Mag. **30**(3), 83–98 (2013)
6. Chung, F.R.: Spectral graph theory, vol. 92 (1997)
7. Singh, A., Dutta, M.K., Jennane, R., Lespessailles, E.: Classification of the trabecular bone structure of osteoporotic patients using machine vision. Comput. Biol. Med. **91**, 148–158 (2017)
8. Ktena, S.I., et al.: Distance metric learning using graph convolutional networks: application to functional brain networks. In: Descoteaux, M., Maier-Hein, L., Franz, A., Jannin, P., Collins, D.L., Duchesne, S. (eds.) MICCAI 2017. LNCS, vol. 10433, pp. 469–477. Springer, Cham (2017). https://doi.org/10.1007/978-3-319-66182-7_54
9. Heinsfeld, A.S., Franco, A.R., Craddock, R.C., Buchweitz, A., Meneguzzi, F.: Identification of autism spectrum disorder using deep learning and the abide dataset. NeuroImage Clin. **17**, 16–23 (2018)
10. Kazeminejad, A., Sotero, R.C.: Topological properties of resting-state fmri functional networks improve machine learning-based autism classification. Front. Neurosci. **12**, 1018 (2019)
11. Craddock, C., et al.: Towards automated analysis of connectomes: the configurable pipeline for the analysis of connectomes (C-PAC). Front. Neuroinformatics **42** (2013)
12. Glasser, M.F., et al.: A multi-modal parcellation of human cerebral cortex. Nature **536**(7615), 171–178 (2016)

13. Huang, W., Bolton, T.A.W., Medaglia, J.D., Bassett, D.S., Ribeiro, A., Van De Ville, D.: A graph signal processing perspective on functional brain imaging. Proc. IEEE **106**(5), 868–885 (2018)
14. Huang, W., Goldsberry, L., Wymbs, N.F., Grafton, S.T., Bassett, D.S., Ribeiro, A.: Graph frequency analysis of brain signals. IEEE J. Sel. Top. Signal Process. **10**(7), 1189–1203 (2016)
15. Varoquaux, G., Baronnet, F., Kleinschmidt, A., Fillard, P., Thirion, B.: Detection of brain functional-connectivity difference in post-stroke patients using group-level covariance modeling. In: Jiang, T., Navab, N., Pluim, J.P.W., Viergever, M.A. (eds.) MICCAI 2010. LNCS, vol. 6361, pp. 200–208. Springer, Heidelberg (2010). https://doi.org/10.1007/978-3-642-15705-9_25
16. Sato, J.R., Calebe Vidal, M., de Siqueira Santos, S., Brauer Massirer, K., Fujita, A.: Complex network measures in autism spectrum disorders. IEEE/ACM Trans. Comput. Biol. Bioinform. **15**(2), 581–587 (2018)

Radiomic and Dosiomic Profiling of Paediatric Medulloblastoma Tumours Treated with Intensity Modulated Radiation Therapy

Cinzia Talamonti[1,2,3]([✉]) [iD], Stefano Piffer[1,2], Daniela Greto[3],
Monica Mangoni[1,3], Antonio Ciccarone[4], Paolo Dicarolo[4],
Maria Evelina Fantacci[5,6], Franco Fusi[1], Piernicola Oliva[7,8],
Letizia Palumbo[5,6], Claudio Favre[4], Lorenzo Livi[1,3],
Stefania Pallotta[1,2,3], and Alessandra Retico[6]

[1] University of Florence, Piazza San Marco, 50100 Florence, Italy
cinzia.talamonti@unifi.it
[2] National Institute for Nuclear Physics (INFN), Firenze Division,
Largo Bruno Pontecorvo 3, 56127 Florence, Italy
[3] Azienda Ospedaliera Universitaria Careggi, Largo Brambilla 3,
50134 Florence, Italy
[4] Azienda Ospedaliera Universitaria Meyer, Viale Gaetano Pieraccini, 24,
50139 Florence, Italy
[5] University of Pisa, Largo Bruno Pontecorvo 3, 56127 Pisa, Italy
[6] National Institute for Nuclear Physics (INFN), Pisa Division,
Largo Bruno Pontecorvo 3, 56127 Pisa, Italy
[7] University of Sassari, Via Vienna, 2, 07100 Sassari, Italy
[8] National Institute for Nuclear Physics (INFN), Cagliari Division,
SP Sestu km 0.7, 09042 Monserrato, CA, Italy

Abstract. The aim of this work is to describe the state of progress of a study developed in the framework of AIM (Artificial Intelligence in Medicine). It is a project funded by INFN, Italy, and it involves researchers from INFN, Hospital Meyer and Radiotherapy Unit of University of Florence. The aim of the proposed study is to apply a retrospective exploratory MR-CT-based radiomics and dosiomic analysis based on emerging machine-learning technologies, to investigate imaging biomarkers of clinical outcomes in paediatric patients affected by medulloblastoma, from images. Features from MR-CT scans will be associated with overall survival, recurrence-free survival, and loco-regional recurrence-free survival after intensity modulated radiotherapy. Dosimetric analysis data will be integrated with the objective of increase predictive value. This approach could have a large impact for precision medicine, as radiomic biomarkers are non-invasive and can be applied to imaging data that are already acquired in clinical settings.

Keywords: Dosiomic · Medulloblastoma · Radiomic

M. Vento and G. Percannella (Eds.): CAIP 2019 Workshops, CCIS 1089, pp. 56–64, 2019.
https://doi.org/10.1007/978-3-030-29930-9_6

1   Introduction

In the rapidly expanding field of precision medicine there is very high demand of predictive models in order to choose treatments tailored on the patient. Medical imaging provides valuable information which can be employed through computer assisted interpretation. Radiomics analysis can extract many imaging features quantitatively, and therefore offers a cost-effective and non-invasive approach for individual medicine. Several studies have shown the predictive and diagnostic ability of radiomic features in different kinds of cancer, using various medical imaging modalities, such as PET, MRI and CT. It is also demonstrated that radiomic features can be correlated with the overall survival probability. Along with texture analysis, biomedical research has been boosted by the evidence of a predictive role of numerous molecular biomarkers. At the same time, the evolution of the diagnostic tools, extensively relying on numerical methods and computer science technologies, is giving raise to large digital datasets that can be exploited to extract an increasingly large number of variables.

The aim of this work is to describe the progress of a study developed in the framework of the AIM (Artificial Intelligence in Medicine) project funded by INFN, which involves physicists from INFN and clinicians and medical physicists from Hospital Meyer and Radiotherapy Unit of University of Florence. The present work is developed within the Predictive Models work-package of AIM, whose purpose is to investigate the predictive role of texture analysis and clinical data for the treatment outcome after intensity modulated radiotherapy (IMRT) of paediatric patients affected by central nervous system tumours (CNS). The data used for the study are provided by a radiomic profiling of patients affected by medulloblastoma at paediatric Meyer Hospital and treated with Intensity Modulated Radiation Therapy in the Radiotherapy Unit. The main focus was on correlations between dose distribution to risk organs and brain toxicity and/or possible recurrences.

A retrospective study has been made collecting about 70 paediatric patients that underwent radiotherapy treatments from 2015 to 2018. Pre-treatment and follow-up CT and MRI studies were considered. In particular, the available examinations were: diffusion MR images with contrast medium, CT images used for radiotherapy treatment planning, and dosimetric data for radiotherapy treatments. The most important clinical data for the study were: survival, type of tumour, degree of differentiation, malignancy, histological report, type of therapeutic pathway dose delivered, fractionation, chemotherapy regiments and drugs. Radiomic approach was also used to extract the "dosiomic" features.

The potentially breaking-through aim of the proposed project is to enable the identification of otherwise extremely difficult to spot correlations among imaging features, dose distribution and clinical response to IMRT. This project relies on some very strong starting points: availability of a substantial amount of homogeneous patient data; prompt availability of already acquired data and easy to recruit patients for future studies; centralized imaging and data analysis that improve the value of the study. The project is very relevant in predicting the outcome of the treatments and it is crucial to enable the clinicians to judge the most appropriate therapies for patients. This project aims at exploring a technology which has the potential to be far more reaching than the scope of this specific study and promises to have broad impact in the domain of precisely patient-tuned treatments.

2 Study Population

Medulloblastoma (MB) is the most common malignant brain tumour in paediatric population. MB accounts for 20% of primary neoplasm of central nervous system (CNS) in children [1]. The more common location is the cerebellum with a high incidence of spread in spinal cord. The most important factors influencing the prognosis are age at diagnosis, histology, metastases at diagnosis and residual tumour after surgery. Medulloblastoma with residual tumour > 1.5 cm^3, metastases at diagnosis and anaplastic large cell histological subtypes are classified high risk, patients without the previous characteristics are classified as standard risk [2]. The clinical outcome of patients differs from the risk class, the 5-year survival rate of standard risk patients is 80% and 60% in case of high-risk disease [3]. The standard treatment is a multi-modality approach involving surgery, radiotherapy and chemotherapy. Patients younger than 3–5 years are treated with surgery and chemotherapy, radiotherapy is avoided due to the high risk of late sequalae related to radiotherapy treatment in this young subpopulation [4]. Surgery is fundamental in medulloblastoma treatment, the aim of the surgical approach is to reach the maximal resection but, in some cases, due to the tumour location and the high risk of neurological sequalae, a complete surgery resection is not possible. After surgery, craniospinal irradiation (CSI) is delivered and followed by a further focused delivery (boost) to the posterior fossa (PF) or in last years to the surgical bed. An additional radiotherapy boost is delivered to residual disease and metastatic sites. Radiotherapy doses and fractionations depend from the risk class varying from 23.4–39 Gy (1.3–1.8 Gy/fraction, 1 or 2 fractions/day) for the CSI and 50.4–59.4 Gy for the boost. Multidrug chemotherapy is administered before, concomitant and after radiotherapy in high risk patients, after radiotherapy in standard risk patients [5]. Patient staging is performed with brain and spinal MRI with gadolinium and cerebrospinal fluid (CSF) analysis at diagnosis. A brain and spinal MRI with contrast is performed after surgery to assess the risk class and, during follow up, to early detect recurrence or radiological changes due to treatments at 1 month and every three months thereafter at the end of the multimodal treatment [6].

2.1 Clinical Data

Selection criteria to include patients in the study were the availability of MR imaging before and after radiation treatment, and a minimum of one year of follow up after the treatment. Risk class was assessed recording age at diagnosis (ranging between 3–21 years), radiological staging, histological subtypes. All patients underwent a staging brain and spinal MRI with contrast to assess any surgical residual or metastases, and in absence of macroscopic metastases, CSF analysis was performed to exclude microscopic spinal disease dissemination. Surgical report was recorded, the administration of chemotherapy and the association to radiotherapy was also reported. Radiotherapy schedules and irradiation volumes were finally recorded. Clinical and neurological evaluation was performed periodically at diagnosis, after surgery, during chemotherapy and radiotherapy administration and during follow up early and late sequelae were recorded. Disease control was defined according to RECIST criteria: stable disease (SD), progressive disease (PD), partial response (PR), complete response (CR) and distant progressive disease in case of a new lesion occurrence. CTCAE criteria v.4.0 scored toxicity. Survival was defined from the time of surgery to last follow up or death. Death was defined as due to: tumour related in case of tumour progression, neurological death due to neurological deterioration or due to other causes.

3 Imaging

MR imaging plays an essential role in the management of paediatric patients with medulloblastoma, since it can be integrated in the therapeutic strategies due to its capacity of studying the tumour non-invasively and non-destructively repeatedly. It has the capability of detecting soft-tissue contrast by providing superior anatomic information and, moreover different MR image sequences are sensitive to key components of tumour physiology and can distinguish regions of the tumour which contains different environments. Patient enrolled in this study underwent several MR imaging sessions. In each session many sequences were acquired (T1W TSE, T1W TSE MDC, T2W TSE, T2W FLAIR) to exploit various biomedical properties of the tumour more effectively than other imaging modalities. Necrosis and solid tumour can be visually distinguished using T1W TSE MDC, whilst T2W TSE can be used to estimate cellular density and the presence of oedema.

4 Dose Distribution Information

Many studies have already considered the radiomic analysis of the features extracted from the MRI as this imaging technique is considered the landmark in CNS lesions diagnosis and monitoring [7]. Moreover, since in the medulloblastoma course of treatment, radiotherapy is a well-established step, in addition to surgery and chemotherapy, the innovative idea behind this study is to introduce the radiomic analysis also on the images of the dose distribution. Thereby radiomic approach is used to extract the spatial features from dose distribution (dosiomic features) in order to predict the response to radiotherapy treatment and the related side effects or the development of distant metastases.

All patients enrolled in this study, were treated with Helical Tomotherapy. Treatment plans were computed using TomoHelical treatment planning system. The planning CT had slices 3 mm thick. The dose was prescribed to cover at least 95% of the planning target volume (PTV). A manual outlining of the target and of the Organ At Risk (OAR) was performed by an expert radiotherapist on the treatment planning CT.

The dosiomic features, such as mean dose, ROI volume within which the dose is greater than x Gy (V_x), entropy, uniformity and spatial dose gradient, have been extracted from the RT-DOSE DICOM images.

The basic idea is to bring out two important aspects that can help researchers to better understand the potential of the dosiomic features analysis. Firstly, medical judgement of images consists typically in a qualitative and subjective description of changes due to contrast differences. The radiomic analysis provides a huge amount of information and has proven to be very useful in the treatment of cancer patients, providing quantitative features that help to reduce discretion and subjectivity [8]. Secondly, dosimetric variables do not consider all the information available in the dose distribution. For instance, the spatial information is not included in the Dose Volume Histogram (DVH) curve and it is founded only on discrete point data such as V_x [9].

For these reasons, it is reasonable to hypothesize that if the radiomic features will be used for boost planning and the dosiomic features will be exploited properly, the prediction ability of the therapeutic responses should be further improved. This capacity coming from the analysis of both radiomic and dosiomic features, could be implemented in the future in the TCP, NTCP and patient's survival models.

5 Statistical Analysis and Machine Learning

The multimodal data available for each subject contain a large amount of complementary information potentially useful to predict patient's outcome [10, 11]. A data driven predictive model is set up, based on the exploitation of radiomics features extracted from radiological images, including the pre-treatment MRI and CT images, and the dose distribution of the administered radiotherapy treatment plan. Quantitative features are extracted from patients' images and dose distributions and encoded in vectors of features. Statistical data analysis to compare the distributions of quantitative features between the cohort of patients who have developed a treatment-related toxicity and the control sample are implemented. In addition, machine learning-based predictive models are trained on labelled data patterns to find hidden relationships among complex and heterogeneous data samples, such as the ones considered in this analysis. Binary classification models are generally implemented in cases where the aim is to assign the correct class membership to a new example, according for example to the occurrence of tumour recurrences or of treatment-related toxicity. Once the model is trained to recognize the relevant features that can correctly predict the data labels, and the accuracy of the classifier shows satisfactory performance, the classification system can be validated on data of new, previously unseen, examples to make prediction about the possibility of developing a treatment-related toxicity.

The data analysis pipeline is schematically represented in Fig. 1, and can be summarized in the following steps. The images of the multimodal data sample are processed by a set of algorithms suitable to extract radiomics features, which are stored into vectors, whose entries encode characteristics extracted from the different image modalities available for this analysis. The clinical labels (e.g. the occurrence of tumour recurrences or of treatment-related toxicity), as available through the clinical follow-up of patients, are necessary to build a fully annotated data sample to train the classifier. As a very large number of descriptive features can be extracted from patients' images and dose distributions, it is a fundamental step of our analysis to identify the most relevant set of features to be used in the predictive models. To this purpose, three different approaches will be followed and compared: the a priori selection of a limited number of features, which are supposed to be the most informative for the classification problem, due to the fact that they are related to image texture properties and dose homogeneity in the regions of interest; a data driven feature selection, which is carried out either performing a statistical between-group comparison of each feature to identify the most relevant ones, or feature reduction techniques to be included within the classifier training, as described below. Even after feature selection procedures, the number of radiomics features to explore may be of the same order of magnitude of the available number of subjects in the cohort. Thus, a cross-validation scheme will be adopted to evaluate the classifier performance. In particular, the leave-one-out cross validation (LOO-CV) method is implemented, as it provides a non-biased estimate of the classification performance the system would show when trained on all available data patterns. Within the LOO-CV, the classifier performances are evaluated according to standard figures of merit, e.g. the sensitivity and specificity values, the accuracy and the Area Under the Receiver Operating Characteristic (ROC) curve (AUC).

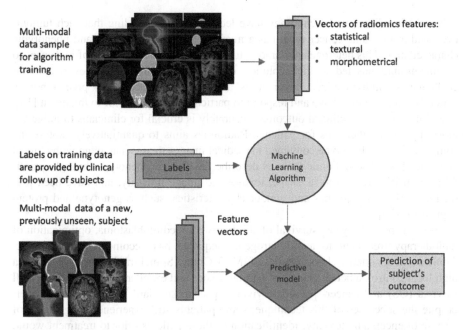

Fig. 1. Schematic representation of the Radiomics study based on machine learning.

The training phase of the machine-learning classifier relies on the comparison between kernel-based methods, e.g. Support Vector Machines (SVM) [12], implemented analogously to the analysis of regional features of tissues reported in [13], and different neural networks architectures (e.g. a three-layer feed-forward classifier) [14], implemented either for the analysis of image descriptive features, as reported in [15], or for a voxel-wise analysis, as reported in [16]. The first category of methods, the kernel-based ones, especially in case linear kernels are implemented, have the valuable advantage of allowing a straightforward identification of the images features which are more responsible for the two-class separation. This property facilitates the selection of relevant features, as it enables the implementation of the Recursive Feature Elimination (RFE) method [17], and thus, a dimensionality reduction.

In addition, within the classifier training phase, the predictive power of the different groups of features extracted from the different sets of images will be compared against each other. The more informative subset of features is retained for the rest of the analysis. Once the classifier is trained and its performances have been assessed, it can be used to predict labels on new examples, as sketched in Fig. 1.

The technical implementation of the analysis pipeline takes advantage of the open-source python programming language (https://www.python.org), including a specific package (PyRadiomics) for the extraction of radiomics features from medical images [18].

6 Conclusion

Advances in science and technology have led to the understanding that each tumour, even within the same cancer type, has a myriad of distinct genotypic and phenotypic characteristics. This heterogeneity among tumours results in a spectrum of responses to treatments and has led to the evolution of precision medicine. However, a major challenge for individualized treatment is the inability to accurately predict how a patient's disease will behave and respond to particular therapies prior to treatment [19]. The ability to predict clinical outcomes accurately is crucial for clinicians to judge the most appropriate therapies for patients. Radiomics aims to quantitatively capture the complex tumour phenotype contained in medical images to associate them with clinical outcomes [19]. The radiomic features describe the tumour phenotype through quantifying properties related to its shape, texture and image intensity, and have been predictive of clinical outcomes and tumour characteristics, such as genotype and protein expression [20].

With increased 5 years survival of children with medulloblastoma, optimization of radiotherapy treatment to avoid iatrogenic sequelae has become a primary issue. Clinical and dosimetric characteristics of IMRT Cranio Spinal Irradiation have shown a high local control, a better sparing of normal tissues and excellent local control, overall survival (OS) and cancer-specific survival respect to standard 3DRT [21]. However, despite the successes of this technique, some patients still experience progression of disease or encephalic toxicity. Identification of these patients prior to treatment would allow augmentation of their therapeutic approach with addition of systemic therapy and/or radiation dose intensification to reduce disease relapse rates and increase OS. Therefore, a strategy that can correctly stratify patients at high risk of failure is needed.

Radiomic analysis of MR-CT scans represents an interesting way to identify imaging predictors of clinical outcomes patients treated with SBRT [22–24]. Systemic inflammation has been associated with the outcome of patients with malignancies. Cancer can induce local or systemic inflammation and cancer-related inflammation can influence cell proliferation, cell survival, angiogenesis, tumour cell migration, invasion and metastasis of adaptive immunity [25].

The aim of this study is to apply a retrospective exploratory MR-CT-based radiomics and dosiomic analysis based on emerging machine-learning technologies, to investigate imaging biomarkers of clinical outcomes in paediatric patients from pre-treatment images. Features from MR-CT scans were associated with OS, recurrence-free survival, and loco-regional recurrence-free survival after IMRT. Dosimetric analysis data were integrated with the objective of increase predictive value. This approach could have a large impact for precision medicine, as radiomic biomarkers are non-invasive and can be applied to imaging data that are already acquired in clinical settings. The retrospective study includes all the paediatric patients treated at the Radiotherapy Unit. Strengths of our analysis are the number of available patients, rapid data collection due to the retrospective design of the study, centralized imaging and data analysis that improve value of data analysis.

This project started on January 2019 and at present effort is being made in creating a common database collecting images and clinical data of paediatric patients, which are archived both at Meyer paediatric Hospital, and in the Radiotherapy section of the University of Florence. In the meantime, we also started to analyse a subset of data with software developed ad hoc by the INFN group for the selection of the most relevant features. To obtain features with a high prognostic power a very large and homogeneous database is needed. This request is difficult to fulfil while reducing and standardizing the database, and a degree of heterogeneity remains due to the fact that each patient is an entity independent from the others. Each person has their own peculiarities and facets, also because a 'personalized medicine' is increasingly aimed, where treatment is tailored on the basis of specific characteristics of the patients and their disease.

This approach could have a large impact for precision medicine, as radiomic and dosiomic are non-invasive and can be applied to imaging data and clinical data that are already acquired in clinical settings. The results of this project will be far more reaching than the specific use case here described and pave the way to the development of therapies more and more tailored on every single patient.

References

1. RARECAREnet. http://www.rarecarenet.eu/rarecarenet. Accessed 19 June 2019
2. Lassaletta, A.: Medulloblastoma in infants: the never-ending challenge. Lancet Oncol. **19**(6), 720–721 (2018)
3. Gatta, G.: Childhood cancer survival in Europe 1999–2007: results of EUROCARE-5 – a population-based study. Lancet Oncol. **15**(1), 35–47 (2014)
4. Ater, J.L.: MOPP chemotherapy without irradiation as primary postsurgical therapy for brain tumors in infants and young children. J. Neurooncol. **32**(3), 243–252 (1997)
5. Massimino, M.: Childhood medulloblastoma. Crit. Rev. Oncol./Hematol. **105**, 35–51 (2016)
6. Noble, D.J.: Fast imaging employing steady-state acquisition (FIESTA) MRI to investigate cerebrospinal fluid (CSF) within dural reflections of posterior fossa cranial nerves. Br. J. Radiol. **89**(1067), 1–10 (2016)
7. Chaddad, A.: Radiomics in glioblastoma: current status and challenges facing clinical implementation. Front. Oncol. **9**(374), 1–9 (2019)

8. Gardin, I.: Radiomics: principles and radiotherapy applications. Crit. Rev. Oncol./Hematol. **138**, 44–50 (2019)
9. Liang, B.: Dosiomics: extracting 3D spatial features from dose distribution to predict incidence of radiation pneumonitis. Front. Oncol. **9**(269), 1–7 (2019)
10. Gillies, R.J.: Radiomics: images are more than pictures, they are data. Radiology **278**(2), 563–577 (2016)
11. Lambin, P.: Radiomics: extracting more information from medical images using advanced feature analysis. Eur. J. Cancer **48**(4), 441–446 (2012)
12. Vapnik, V.: The Nature of Statistical Learning Theory. Springer, Berlin (1995). https://doi.org/10.1007/978-1-4757-2440-0
13. Gori, I.: Gray matter alterations in young children with autism spectrum disorders: comparing morphometry at the voxel and regional level. J. Neuroimaging **25**(6), 866–874 (2015)
14. Haykin, S.: Neural Networks: A Comprehensive Foundation, 2nd edn. Prentice Hall, Upper Saddle River (1998)
15. Delogu, P.: Characterization of mammographic masses using a gradient-based segmentation algorithm and a neural classifier. Comput. Biol. Med. **37**(10), 1479–1491 (2007)
16. Retico, A.: A voxel-based neural approach (VBNA) to identify lung nodules in the ANODE09 study. In: Proceedings of SPIE – The International Society for Optical Engineering, vol. 7260, pp. 1–8 (2009)
17. Retico, A.: Predictive models based on support vector machines: whole-brain versus regional analysis of structural MRI in the Alzheimer's disease. J. Neuroimaging **25**(4), 552–563 (2015)
18. Van Griethuysen, J.J.M.: Computational radiomics system to decode the radiographic phenotype. Can. Res. **77**(21), 104–107 (2017)
19. Lambin, P.: Predicting outcomes in radiation oncology–multifactorial decision support systems. Nat. Rev. Clin. Oncol. **10**(1), 27–40 (2013)
20. Huynh, E.: Associations of radiomic data extracted from static and respiratory-gated CT scans with disease recurrence in lung cancer patients treated with SBRT. PLoS ONE **12**(1), 1–17 (2017)
21. Meroni, S.: Clinical and dosimetric issues of VMAT craniospinal irradiation for paediatric medulloblastoma. Radiother. Oncol. **119**, S408 (2016)
22. Fried, D.V.: Prognostic value and reproducibility of pretreatment CT texture features in stage III non-small cell lung cancer. Int. J. Radiat. Oncol. Biol. Phys. **90**(4), 834–842 (2014)
23. Mattonen, S.A.: Early prediction of tumor recurrence based on CT texture changes after stereotactic ablative radiotherapy (SABR) for lung cancer. Med. Phys. **41**(3), 1–14 (2014)
24. Huang, K.: High-risk CT features for detection of local recurrence after stereotactic ablative radiotherapy for lung cancer. Radiother. Oncol. **109**(1), 51–57 (2013)
25. Mantovani, A.: Cancer-related inflammation. Nature **454**(7203), 436–444 (2008)

May Radiomic Data Predict Prostate Cancer Aggressiveness?

Danila Germanese[4]([⊠]), Sara Colantonio[4], Claudia Caudai[5],
Maria Antonietta Pascali[4], Andrea Barucci[2], Nicola Zoppetti[2],
Simone Agostini[1], Elena Bertelli[1], Laura Mercatelli[1], Vittorio Miele[1],
and Roberto Carpi[3]

[1] Azienda Ospedaliero Universitaria Careggi,
Largo G. Brambilla 3, 50134 Florence, Italy
[2] "Nello Carrara" Institute of Applied Physics, IFAC-CNR,
via Madonna del Piano 10, 50019 Florence, Italy
[3] Azienda USL Toscana Centro,
Piazza Santa Maria Nuova 1, 50019 Florence, Italy
[4] ISTI-CNR, Pisa, Italy
{danila.germanese,sara.colantonio}@isti.cnr.it
[5] ITB-CNR, Pisa, Italy

Abstract. Radiomics can quantify tumor phenotypic characteristics non-invasively by defining a signature correlated with biological information. Thanks to algorithms derived from computer vision to extract features from images, and machine learning methods to mine data, Radiomics is the perfect case study of application of Artificial Intelligence in the context of precision medicine. In this study we investigated the association between radiomic features extracted from multi-parametric magnetic resonance imaging (mp-MRI)of prostate cancer (PCa) and the tumor histologic subtypes (using Gleason Score) using machine learning algorithms, in order to identify which of the mp-MRI derived radiomic features can distinguish high and low risk PCa.

Keywords: Machine learning · Artificial intelligence · Radiomics ·
Image processing · Computer vision · Prostate cancer

1 Introduction

In the paradigm of precision medicine, Radiomics is an - omic science, aiming at the improvement of diagnostic, prognostic, and predictive accuracy [1,2].

Mining quantitative images features from clinical imaging, Radiomics uses advanced quantitative features to objectively and quantitatively describe tumor phenotypes. These features can be extracted from medical images using advanced mathematical algorithms [3] to discover tumor characteristics that may not be appreciated by the naked eye. Radiomic features can provide richer information about intensity, shape, size or volume, and texture of tumor phenotype that is

© Springer Nature Switzerland AG 2019
M. Vento and G. Percannella (Eds.): CAIP 2019 Workshops, CCIS 1089, pp. 65–75, 2019.
https://doi.org/10.1007/978-3-030-29930-9_7

distinct or complementary to that provided by clinical reports, laboratory test results, and genomic or proteomic assays.

Radiomics may thus provide great potential to capture important phenotypic information, such as intratumoral heterogeneity, subsequently providing valuable information for personalised therapy [4–7].

In this work, we aimed at implementing a machine learning-based automatic classification of PCa aggressiveness (Low-grade PCa vs. High-grade PCa) by using mp-MRI-based radiomic features. In particular we will focus on two different MRI maps, T2-weighted (T2w) MR imaging, and the Apparent Diffusion Coefficient (ADC) from diffusion-weighted MR imaging (DWI), both being valuable and well established parameters for differentiating PCa aggressiveness [17,26–28].

PCa is among the most common cancers and the second leading cause of cancer-specific mortality among Western males, imposing a huge economic and social burden [8]. In general, patients with PCa and a Gleason Score[1] (GS) $<=$ $3 + 4$ (Low-grade PCa) have better survival rates, lower biochemical recurrence rate and lower prostate cancer-specific mortality in comparison to the patients with GS $>= 4+3$ (High-grade PCa) [9]. As a consequence, the early grading and stratification of PCa aggressiveness play a key role in the therapy management and in the evaluation of patient long-term survival.

Nevertheless, PCa aggressiveness assessed by biopsy may result in an incorrect diagnosis, in addition to patient discomfort. Moreover, GS evaluated from biopsies may differ from that assessed following radical prostatectomy due, for example, to an incomplete sampling [10–12]. Therefore, non-invasive and robust radiological image-based techniques that can help the clinicians in the evaluation of PCa aggressiveness are needed to enhance the quality of both clinical outcomes and patient care.

The role of machine learning techniques in analysing radiomic features have been investigated in many studies, e.g. for the discrimination of PCa from non-cancer prostate tissue [13–17], or in the classification of PCa with different GS [18,19], or in the assessment of PCa aggressiveness [20]. In particular, texture-based radiomic features showed effectiveness in discriminating between cancer and non-cancer prostate tissue [21,22] and in the assessment of PCa aggressiveness [23,24].

Despite a huge amount of works it is important to highlight that there is not a unanimous consent about the specific radiomic signature that is most effective in distinguishing PCa aggressiveness. In our opinion the origins of this failure can be sought in the lack of standardised and robust data, in the use of

---

[1] The Gleason grading system is used to help evaluate the prognosis of men with prostate cancer using samples from a prostate biopsy. The pathologist looks at how the cancer cells are arranged in the prostate and assigns a score on a scale of 3 to 5 from 2 different locations. Please note the notation: the first number is the most common grade in all the samples, while the second number is the highest grade of what's left. Gleason Score = the most common grade + the highest other grade in the samples.

small dataset which are usually unable to explain all the variability of the real samples. A solution to this phenomenon could be obtained using shared imaging biobanks. Datasets originating from a single institution can be very useful to test algorithms and to begin to understand which radiomic features can be the most representatives for PCa, but the definition of a radiomic signature with a strong clinical impact requires a different kind of dataset. The dimension of the imaging dataset is obviously directly related to the clinical problem of interest and at to kind of algorithm implemented.

In the presented work, we aimed at implementing a machine learning-based system to automatically classify PCa aggressiveness (Low-grade PCa vs. High-grade PCa). We compared the results obtained using *(i)* the whole set of 851 radiomic features *(first-order statistics, shape-based 3D features, shape-based 2D features, Gray level Cooccurence Matrix features, Gray level Run Length Matrix features, Gray level Size Zone Matrix features, Neighbouring Gray Tone Difference Matrix features, Gray level Dependence Matrix features* and their wavelet transform which yields 8 decompositions per level - all possible combinations of applying either a High or a Low pass filter in each of the three dimensions) and *(ii)* only those calculated on the original image (107, without wavelet filtering); and considering three dataset *(i)* T2w, *(ii)* ADC, *(iii)* T2w + ADC.

The paper is organised as follows: Sect. 2 describes the whole radiomic process (image acquisition, image segmentation, feature extraction and selection, analysis and model building); Sect. 3 reports the achieved results; Sect. 4 concludes the paper.

2   Methods and Materials

2.1   Patient Cohort

This retrospective study involved 125 patients who underwent a 1.5 T mp-MRI and free hand transperineal MRI/US fusion-guided targeted biopsy (MyLab-TM Twice Esaote).

From such cohort of patients, we selected 50 peripheral zone PCa patients for our pilot study, with a PI-RADS score[2] 3–5, corresponding to an intermediate-to-very high probability of malignancy. 57 lesions were biopsied and the histopathological result was as follow: 37 with GS $<= 3+4$, consistent with a less aggressive behaviour of the prostate cancer, and 20 with GS $>= 4+3$.

---

[2] The PI-RADS v2 [25] (Prostate Imaging Reporting & Data System) assessment categories are based on the findings of mp-MRI, combining T2-weighted (T2W), diffusion weighted imaging (DWI) and dynamic contrast-enhanced (DCE) imaging. The PI-RADS assessment category determines the likelihood of clinically significant prostate cancer. A score, ranging from 1 to 5, is given accordingly to each imaging technique, with 1 being most probably benign (clinically significant cancer is highly unlikely to be present) and 5 being high suspicious for malignancy.

2.2 Image Acquisition

In this study all exams were performed using a 1.5 T MR scanner (Magnetom Aera, Siemens Healthcare, Erlangen, Germany) equipped with a pelvic phased-array 32-channels coils (Fig. 1).

Our acquisition protocol included:

- High-resolution T2w sequences in the axial (voxel size $0.6 \times 0.6 \times 3.0 \, mm$), sagittal and coronal planes (voxel size $0.7 \times 0.7 \times 3.0 \, mm$);
- T1w pre-contrast sequence in the axial plane (voxel size $0.8 \times 0.8 \times 5 \, mm$);
- a multi-b DWI (range 0–$2000 \, s/mm^2$, step of $500 \, s/mm^2$, voxel size $0.8 \times 0.8 \times 3 \, mm$) EPI sequence from which corresponding ADC maps were automatically calculated using software on board the Siemens MRI console;
- Dynamic Contrast Enhancement (DCE) assessment with time intensity curves evaluation.

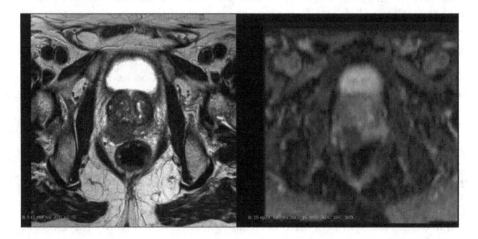

Fig. 1. Example of prostate mp-MRI images. Left: T2w; Right: ADC. Please note that slices are different in the 2 maps

2.3 Image Segmentation

Segmentation was performed on the two most representative sequences for PI-RADS assessment in clinical practice, T2w images and the ADC maps derived from the Diffusion Weighted Imaging (DWI).

Tumor regions were defined by manually drawing ROIs using the 3D Slicer software [29]. For consistency between ROIs, all depicted lesions were strictly segmented with the same criteria and visually validated by three radiologists (with different experience in reporting prostate mp-MRI (15, 5 and 1 year respectively) in consensus, both on T2w images and ADC maps (Figs. 2 and 3).

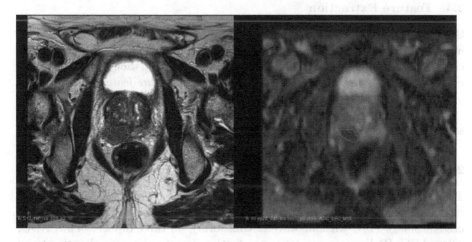

Fig. 2. Example of prostate mp-MRI images ROIs segmentation. Left: T2w; Right: ADC. The green line defines the border of the tumor. (Color figure online)

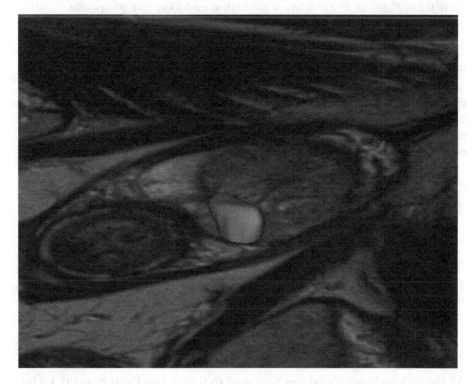

Fig. 3. Example of prostate mp-MRI image 3D segmentation showing the entire tumour volume used for radiomic analysis.

2.4   Feature Extraction

Quantitative features were extracted both from original images and after applying wavelet transform for T2w dataset and for ADC dataset. All the feature classes were computed: *shapes features, first- order statistics features, second-order statistics features* (that included the so called *texture features*) and *higher-order statistics features*, for a total of 851 features.

The features were evaluated using a home-made software based on the open-source python package pyradiomics [30].

2.5   Feature Selection and Classification

The analyses, implemented on MATLAB® R2018 platform, were carried out by considering the whole set of features (851) and only those calculated on the original image (107, without wavelet transform), on three dataset: T2w, ADC, T2w+ADC. Radiomics raw data were firstly normalized across all patients by using quantile normalization.

Then, for each dataset, a correlation analysis was run to detect redundancy. Pearson's correlation coefficient was calculated, and one feature was dropped from those pairs of features showing high correlation (>0.95, p-value <0.05) and, hence, more linear dependence.

A feed-forward feature selection method was applied to select the most discriminative radiomic features. A predictive model was devised to distinguish low-grade (GS $<= 3 + 4$) from intermediate/high-grade (GS $>= 4 + 3$) PCa. A non-linear Support Vector Machine (SVM) was used as the classifier. Starting from an empty feature set, the implemented selection method created candidate feature subsets by sequentially adding each of the features not yet selected. At each step, 10-fold cross-validation was applied to get the prediction accuracy for each candidate feature subset. The process was repeated until the criterion value (that is, the mis-classification error) reached the global minimum.

3   Results

3.1   Radiomic Signatures Building

In Table 1, the built radiomic signatures are shown for each dataset (T2w, ADC, T2w+ADC) and according to the set of features that was considered for the analysis, that means, the whole set of 851 features (F_{851}) and the features computed only on the original image (F_{107}).

3.2   Diagnostic Performance of Radiomic Signatures

All the built radiomic signatures were used to train a non-linear Support Vector Machine (SVM) classifier. It was trained on 40 cases (26 GS $<= 3 + 4$ and 14 GS $>= 4 + 3$) and tested on the remaining 17 (11 GS $<= 3 + 4$ and 6 GS $>= 4 + 3$).

Table 1. The computed radiomic signatures and criterion values (CV) for each dataset.

	F_{851}	F_{107}
T2w	wavelet-LHL glszm Zone Entropy	orig. first ord. Total Energy
	wavelet-LHH glcm Joint Entr.	orig. glszm Size Zone Non Unif. Normal.
	wavelet-HLL glszm Size Zone Non Unif.	orig. shape Max. 2D Diameter Row
	original glcm Idmn	original glcm Idmn
	wavelet-LHL first ord. Root Mean Sq.	orig. ngtdm Strength
	orig. glcm Sum Entropy	orig. gldm Large Dep. High Gray Lev. Emph.
	wavelet-LLH first ord. Entr.	orig. glrlm Long Run High Gray Lev. Emph.
		orig. glszm Size Zone Non Unif.
		orig. gldm Dependence Non Unif. Normal.
		orig. first ord. Energy
		orig. glcm Correlation
		orig. glcm Idm
		orig. glcm Sum Entropy
	CV: 0.086	CV: 0.069
ADC	wavelet-LHH glrlm Run Len. Non Unif.	orig. first ord. Entr.
	wavelet-LHH first ord. Tot. Energy	orig. ngtdm Contrast
	wavelet-LLL glcm Correlation	orig. shape Minor Axis Length
	wavelet-LHH first ord. Root Mean Sq.	orig. first order Uniformity
	wavelet-HHL glszm Gray Lev. Non Unif.	orig. ngtdm Complexity
	wavelet-LLL ngtdm Contrast	orig. glcm Contrast
	wavelet-HLL first ord. Root Mean Sq.	orig. glcm Diff. Average
	wavelet-LLH glcm Id	orig. shape Least Axis Length
	wavelet-HLH first ord. 10%	orig. glrlm Long Run High Gray Lev. Emph.
		orig. glcm Joint Entropy
		orig. glrlm High Gray Lev. Run Emph.
		orig. glcm Difference Variance
		orig. gldm Small Dep. Low Gray Lev. Emph.
		orig. glszm Size Zone Non Unif.
	CV: 0.024	CV: 0.155
T2w + ADC	wavelet-HLL glcm Joint Energy	orig. glcm Idmn
	orig. glszm Size Zone Non Unif. Nor.	orig. shape Minor Axis Length
	wavelet-HLL gldm Dep. Non Unif.	orig. ngtdm Complexity
	wavelet-LHH first ord. Tot. En.	orig. glszm Size Zone Non Unif.
	wavelet-HLL glcm Imc1	orig. glcm Diff. Average
	wavelet-LLH glcm Correlation	orig. glcm MCC
	wavelet-HLH first ord. Range	orig. glszm Gray Lev. Non Unif. Normal.
	wavelet-LHL glszm Gray Leve. Non Unif.	orig. first ord. Maximum
	wavelet-LLH glcm Correlation	orig. glrlm Gray Level Non Unif.
	wavelet-HLL gldm Low Gray Lev. Emph.	
	CV: 0.000	CV: 0.053

As shown in Fig. 4, the best performance was obtained with the T2w+ADC radiomic signature built including the wavelet parameters, with an overall accuracy of 94.12%, 100% sensitivity, 90,9% specificity (just one case misclassified).

We obtained in the other cases: 88.23% accuracy (60% sens, 100% spec) for T2w+ADC (9 features without wavelet); 88.23% accuracy (71,42% sens, 83,33% spec) for T2w (7 features with wavelet); 82.35% accuracy (60% sens, 100% spec) for T2w (13 features without wavelet); 94.11% accuracy (80% sens, 100% spec)

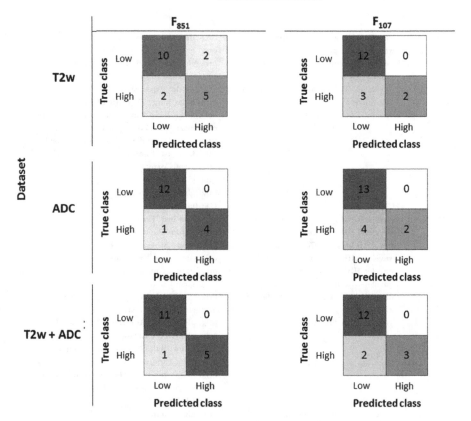

Fig. 4. Confusion matrices for all the investigated cases.

for ADC (9 features with wavelet); 78.94% accuracy (50% sens, 100% spec) for ADC (14 features without wavelet).

4   Conclusion

In this study, we evaluated the potential role of radiomic features in predicting the aggressiveness of prostate cancer compared with bioptic Gleason score. We compared the prediction power of six radiomic signatures, selected from three dataset (T2w MRI-based radiomic features dataset, ADC MRI-based radiomic features dataset, and the combination of both) and using both the whole set of computed features, that integrated also the ones computed on the wavelet transformed images, and the set of features that included the features calculated on the original images only.

The ADC dataset with the whole set of features gave good accuracy in discriminating between high vs low risk PCa. Also, the combination of ADC and

T2w radiomic features, along with the inclusion of wavelet filtering, seemed to add discriminative information to the lesions classification.

The idea would be to ground on the latter result and build a radiomic signature which include both ADC and T2w radiomic features, in accordance with the fact that also PI-RADS assessment uses a combination of mp-MRI T2W and DWI findings. However, a deeper investigation will be carried on a larger, multicentre dataset with a more balanced distribution to confirm such results.

The identification of a robust and validated radiomic signature would be fundamental to move precision medicine forward. Indeed, in combination with other omics data, radiomic signatures can then be used for the development of diagnostic and prognostic models, describing phenotypic patterns connected to biological or clinical end points, aiming at tailoring of the therapies based on patient's needs and at the monitoring of the response to care.

References

1. Lambin, P., et al.: Radiomics: the bridge between medical imaging and personalized medicine. Nat. Rev. Clin. Oncol. **14**, 749 (2017). https://doi.org/10.1038/nrclinonc.2017.141
2. Gillies, R.J., Kinahan, P.E., Hricak, H.: Radiomics: images are more than pictures, they are data. Radiology **278**(2), 563–577 (2016). https://doi.org/10.1148/radiol.2015151169
3. Larue, R.T.H.M., et al.: Influence of gray level discretization on radiomic feature stability for different CT scanners, tube currents and slice thiknesses: a comprehensive phantom study. Acta Oncol. **56**, 1544–1553 (2017)
4. Barucci, A., et al.: Exposing cancer's complexity using radiomics in clinical imaging. An investigation on the role of histogram analysis as imaging biomarker to unravel intra-tumour heterogeneity. In: 2018 IEEE Workshop on Complexity in Engineering (COMPENG), pp. 1–5 (2018). https://doi.org/10.1109/CompEng.2018.8536244
5. Stoyanova, R., et al.: Prostate cancer radiomics and the promise of radiogenomics. Transl. Cancer Res. **5**(4), 432–447 (2016). https://doi.org/10.21037/tcr.2016.06.20
6. Aerts, H.J., Velazquez, E.R., Leijenaar, R.T., Parmar, C., Grossmann, P., Carvalho, S., et al.: Decoding tumour phenotype by noninvasive imaging using a quantitative radiomics approach. Nat. Commun. **5**, 4006 (2014). https://doi.org/10.1038/ncomms5006
7. Avanzo, M., Stancanello, J., El Naga, I.: Beyond imaging: the promise of radiomics. Physica Med. **38**, 122–139 (2017). https://doi.org/10.1016/j.ejmp.2017.05.071
8. Bray, F., et al.: Global cancer statistics 2018: GLOBOCAN estimates of incidence and mortality worldwide for 36 cancers in 185 countries. CA Cancer J. Clin. **68**, 394–424 (2018)
9. Ahmed, H.U., et al.: Transatlantic consensus group on active surveillance and focal therapy for prostate cancer. BJU Int. **109**, 1636–1647 (2012)
10. King, C.R., Long, J.P.: Prostate biopsy grading errors: a sampling problem? Int. J. Cancer **90**, 326–330 (2000)
11. Epstein, J.I., Feng, Z., Trock, B.J., Pierorazio, P.M.: Upgrading and downgrading of prostate cancer from biopsy to radical prostatectomy: incidence and predictive factors using the modified Gleason grading system and factoring in tertiary grades. Eur. Urol. **61**, 1019–1024 (2012)

12. Berglung, R.K., et al.: Pathological upgrading and up staging with immediate repeat biopsy in patients elegible for active surveillance. J. Urol. **180**, 1964–1967 (2008)
13. Peng, Y., et al.: Quantitative analysis of multiparametric prostate MR images: differentiation between prostate cancer and normal tissue and correlation with Gleason score-a computer-aided diagnosis development study. Radiology **267**, 787–796 (2013)
14. Tiwari, P., Viswanath, S., Kurhanewicz, J., Sridhar, A., Madabhushi, A.: Multi-modal wavelet embedding representation for data combination (MaWERiC): integrating magnetic resonance imaging and spectroscopy for prostate cancer detection. NMR Biomed. **25**, 607–619 (2012)
15. Moradi, M., et al.: Multiparametric MRI maps for detection and grading of dominant prostate tumors. J. Magn. Reson. Imaging **35**, 1403–1413 (2012)
16. Barucci, A., et al.: 301. Prostate cancer Radiomics using multiparametric MR imaging: an exploratory study. In: Proceedings of 10th Congress of the Associazione Italiana di Fisica Medica - AIFM. Physica Medica: Eur. J. Med. Phys. **56**, 246. Elsevier (2018). https://doi.org/10.1016/j.ejmp.2018.04.310
17. Mazaheri, Y., et al.: Prostate cancer: identification with combined diffusion weighted MR imaging and 3D 1H MR spectroscopic imaging-correlation with pathologic findings. Radiology **246**, 480–488 (2008)
18. Wibmer, A., et al.: Haralick texture analysis of prostate MRI: Utility for differentiating non-cancerous prostate from prostate cancer and differentiating prostate cancers with different Gleason scores. Eur. Radiol. **25**, 2840–2850 (2015)
19. Fehr, D., et al.: Automatic classification of prostate cancer Gleason scores from multiparametric magnetic resonance images. Proc. Natl. Acad. Sci. USA **112**, 6265–6273 (2015)
20. Chen, T., et al.: Prostate cancer differentiation and aggressiveness: assessment with a radiomic-based model vs. PI-RADS v2. J. Magn. Reson. Imaging **49**, 875–884 (2019). https://doi.org/10.1002/jmri.26243
21. Sidhu, H.S., et al.: Textural analysis of multiparametric MRI detects transition zone prostate cancer. Eur. Radiol. **27**, 1–11 (2017)
22. Khalvati, F., Wong, A., Haider, M.A.: Automated prostate cancer detection via comprehensive multi-parametric magnetic resonance imaging texture feature model. BMC Med. Imaging **15**, 27 (2015)
23. Vignati, A., et al.: Texture features on T2-weighted magnetic resonance imaging: new potential biomarkers for prostate cancer aggressiveness. Phys. Med. Biol. **60**, 2685–2701 (2015)
24. Nketiah, G., et al.: T2-weighted MRI-derived textural features reflect prostate cancer aggressiveness: preliminary results. Eur. Radiol. **27**, 3050–3059 (2016)
25. Weinreb, J.C., et al.: PI-RADS prostate imaging - reporting and data systems: 2015, version 2. Eur. Urol. **69**, 16–40 (2016)
26. Langer, D.L., et al.: Prostate tissue composition and MR measurements: investigating the relationships between ADC, T2, K(trans), v(e), and corresponding histologic features. Radiology **255**, 485–494 (2010)
27. Oto, A., et al.: Diffusion-weighted and dynamic contrast-enhanced MRI of prostate cancer: correlation of quantitative MR parameters with Gleason score and tumor angiogenesis. AJR Am. J. Roentgenol. **197**, 1382–1390 (2011)
28. Nagarajan, M.B., et al.: Classification of small lesions in breast MRI: evaluating the role of dynamically extracted texture features through feature selection. J. Med. Biol. Eng. **33**, 33 (2013)

29. Fedorov, A., et al.: 3D slicer as an image computing platform for the quantitative imaging network. Magn. Reson. Imaging **30**(9), 1323–1341 (2012)
30. van Griethuysen, J.J.M., et al.: Computational radiomics system to decode the radiographic phenotype. Cancer Res. **77**(21), e104–e107 (2017)

Workshop on Deep-Learning Based Computer Vision for UAV (DL-UAV)

Workshop on Deep-Learning Based Computer Vision for UAV

Workshop Description

Unmanned aerial vehicles (UAV) is an emerging technological paradigm for visual data acquisition to facilitate a variety of applications. The visual data acquired from airborne devices such as UAV pose unique challenges to the existing computer vision methodologies. With UAV based services set to be a 50 billion USD industry by 2023, and artificial intelligence rapidly gaining ground, intelligent UAV systems are to be the next disruptive technology. Indeed, some smart UAV already exist and soon they will become widespread thanks to recent advances in machine learning. Algorithms based on deep learning will undoubtedly play a crucial role in empowering application domains and services in the field of agriculture, remote sensing, urban and forest terrain modeling, construction, public safety, and crowd management. Photogrammetry and image stitching tools comprehensively capture terrain and landscapes to generate geographical maps that enable different kinds of UAV imagery analysis. The resolution and perspective angle at which terrains and objects are captured by an UAV, however, pose new challenges to the existing computer vision algorithms that are largely trained on conventional ground based imagery. There is therefore a new requirement to address the unique challenges posed by the use of intelligent algorithms either embedded on board of a UAV, or remotely controlling the movement and sensors mounted on the UAV to capture imagery for wireless transmission or post-flight processing. The DL-UAV workshop offers a platform for researchers working on addressing challenges and developing solutions for aerial imagery analysis to disseminate and share pertaining research.

The first edition of the Workshop on Deep-learning based computer vision for UAV in conjunction with the 18th international Conference on Computer Analysis of Images and Patterns (CAIP 2019) was held in Salerno, Italy. The workshop program included a keynote talk, followed by oral presentations of the accepted papers, and was attended by around 15 people.

The workshop received 7 submissions from authors belonging to various countries. After a detailed, single-review process 5 submissions were accepted for presentation and publication at the workshop proceedings. The accepted papers were themed to address unique challenges related to aerial imagery analysis and several of them proposed potential solutions. The discussions presented included topics on data generation, framework development, practical applications, and findings of extended projects.

The keynote talk on "Reconnaissance Sensor Automation in airborne Manned-Unmanned-Teaming Missions" was given by Peter Stütz, professor of Aeronautical Engineering at the University of the Bundeswehr, Munich.

We would like to thank the Program Committee members of the workshop, and the CAIP conference organizers for their active participation and timely support.

July 2019   Hamideh Kerdegari
                                                                                            Manzoor Razaak

Organization

Chairs

Hamideh Kerdegari   Kingston University London, UK
Manzoor Razaak   Kingston University London, UK

Program Committee

Matthew Broadbent   Lancaster University, UK
Mahdi Maktabdar Oghaz   Kingston University London, UK

Additional Reviewers

Bakthiyar Ahmed
Mahdi Maktabdar Oghaz

Training Deep Learning Models via Synthetic Data: Application in Unmanned Aerial Vehicles

Andreas Kamilaris[1,2]([✉]), Corjan van den Brink[1], and Savvas Karatsiolis[3]

[1] Pervasive Systems Group, Department of Computer Science, University of Twente, Enschede, The Netherlands
a.kamilaris@utwente.nl, g.c.vandenbrink@student.utwente.nl
[2] Research Centre on Interactive Media,
Smart Systems and Emerging Technologies (RISE), Nicosia, Cyprus
a.kamilaris@rise.org.cy
[3] Department of Computer Science, University of Cyprus, Nicosia, Cyprus
skarat01@cs.ucy.ac.cy
https://www.utwente.nl/en/eemcs/ps/
http://www.rise.org.cy/
https://www.cs.ucy.ac.cy

Abstract. This paper describes preliminary work in the recent promising approach of generating synthetic training data for facilitating the learning procedure of deep learning (DL) models, with a focus on aerial photos produced by unmanned aerial vehicles (UAV). The general concept and methodology are described, and preliminary results are presented, based on a classification problem of fire identification in forests as well as a counting problem of estimating number of houses in urban areas. The proposed technique constitutes a new possibility for the DL community, especially related to UAV-based imagery analysis, with much potential, promising results, and unexplored ground for further research.

Keywords: UAV · Deep learning · Generative data · Aerial imagery

1 Introduction

Deep learning (DL) constitutes a recent, modern technique for image processing and data analysis with large potential [21]. DL belongs to the machine learning (ML) computational field and is similar to artificial neural networks (ANN). DL extends ML by adding more "depth" (complexity) into the model, transforming the data using various functions that allow data representation in a hierarchical way, through several abstraction levels. DL seems to be offering better precision results in classification and/or counting computer vision-related problems, in comparison to traditional techniques such as Scalable Vector Machines and Random Forests, according to relevant surveys [10].

© Springer Nature Switzerland AG 2019
M. Vento and G. Percannella (Eds.): CAIP 2019 Workshops, CCIS 1089, pp. 81–90, 2019.
https://doi.org/10.1007/978-3-030-29930-9_8

An advantage of DL is the reduced need of feature engineering (FE). Previously, traditional approaches for image classification were based on hand-engineered features, whose performance affected the results heavily [1]. Although DL does not require FE, it still needs appropriate datasets as input in DL models during learning. These datasets need to be large, to allow DL models to learn the problem elaborately, and expressive, to capture the variation of classes/features that need to be classified/predicted at the model output. An existing problem is the limited availability of such appropriate datasets. This limitation makes DL models sometimes difficult to generalize and to learn the problem well, towards high precision.

Towards addressing this limitation, a recent possibility is the generation of synthetic datasets to train DL models [7,11,17]. Models are trained using synthetic images, and they are then able to classify images of the real world, or count objects encountered in the real-world images, via this transfer learning-based method.

The contribution of this paper is twofold: on one hand, to present state of art research in generating synthetic data for training DL models. On the other hand, to present preliminary work on a classification problem of fire identification in forests and a counting problem of estimating number of houses in urban areas, based on two datasets comprised of aerial photos.

2   Related Work

DL is divided in discriminative and generative models [6]. The former is about predictions/classifications, and the latter about synthesis/generation of data similar to the input datasets. The use of generative data to train DL models is promising, with early attempts in agriculture indicating positive outcomes [10].

Table 1 lists related work in the field of generating training data to train DL models. The year of publication for every paper reveals how modern this technique is. Please note that we avoided adding details about performance metrics and evaluation results for each paper, because each author used different metrics and experimented on different real-world datasets for testing. However, the general conclusion in all papers was that the performance according to the metric(s) used, was better than baseline (i.e. datasets not enhanced with synthetic data) or state-of-art related work.

From Table 1, it is evident that related work has not entered yet the domain of UAV-based imagery analysis. The only exception is Meta-Sim [11], which tries to learn a generative model of synthetic scenes automatically, via probabilistic scene grammars, and then it obtains images and their corresponding ground-truth via a graphics engine. Meta-Sim validates this idea addressing the problem of semantic segmentation of simulated aerial views of simple roadways. Beyond this work, to our knowledge, no other work has focused yet on generative data-based approaches for UAV-based imaging-related applications.

Table 1. Related work in generative data for training DL models.

Year	Purpose	Ref.
2007	Simulating fluorescence microscope images of cell populations for automated image cytometry	[12]
2016	Enhancing soil images coming from X-ray tomography, generating roots to help the model identify the roots from the soils	[3]
2016	Simulating top-down images of overlapping plants on soil background, to classify 23 different weed species and maize	[4]
2016	Generating fully labeled, dynamic, and photo-realistic proxy virtual world, with a focus on objects of interest, e.g. cars	[5]
2016	Generating synthetic data for semantic segmentation of outdoor scenes, for recognizing aspects such as roads, buildings, cars, people, lights etc.	[19]
2016	Automatically generating realistic synthetic images with pixel-level annotations for semantic segmentation	[20]
2017	Creating synthetic images to predict number of tomatoes in the images	[18]
2018	Generating synthetic data to identify melanoma skin cancer	[7]
2018	Synthetic data for 2D bounding box car detection	[16]
2018	Generating 3D scenes of visually realistic houses, ranging from single-room studios to multi-storied houses, equipped with a diverse set of fully labeled 3D objects, textures and scene layout, for teaching an agent to navigate in an unseen 3D environment	[25]
2018	Generating scenes for teaching an artificial agent to execute tasks in a simulated household environment	[17]
2019	(a) Generating data for semantic segmentation of aerial views of roadways (b) Simulating urban scenes for object detection in urban car driving	[11]

3   Methodology

The general methodology followed in this paper is illustrated in Fig. 1. More advanced and recent proposals based on this general methodology will be discussed in Sect. 5. DL models are trained with synthetic data, and then tested with real-world data. The precision/accuracy results are analyzed and compared with the state-of-art related work (if available), and the observations made are given as feedback to the creation process of the synthetic datasets, to become more detailed and complete (e.g. to include some aspects of the real-world data not included originally, but which affect the model's prediction capabilities).

Our approach in synthetic dataset design would be to understand how DL models perform classification, based on the existing real-world datasets (i.e. problem under study for classification or counting). To achieve this, we take advantage of the work in [15], which allows to visualize what happens inside DL models, i.e. which aspects/characteristics of the image are the ones that trigger the final classification. These characteristics could then be used to better design the synthetic datasets, emphasizing on these aspects when creating the simulated images. In this paper, we focused on two different applications:

1. A classification problem of identifying fires in forest areas from aerial photos.

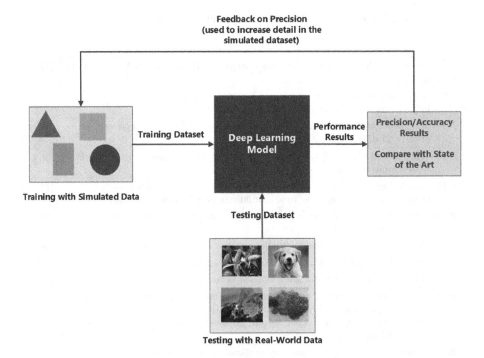

Fig. 1. Basic methodology in generating data for training DL models.

2. A counting problem of estimating number of houses from aerial photos.

The former is useful for UAV which monitor forest areas for fires and smoke, while the latter would be useful for policy-makers who want to understand distribution of houses in urban areas, possibilities for photovoltaic systems, urban gardening in roofs etc.

For the problems under study, the synthetic datasets (used for training the DL model) have been created by means of Python, by using the Python Imaging Library[1] and OpenCV[2]. PIL libraries allow to combine graphics creation, together with programming code and computer logic, using code in order to create dots, lines, rectangles, polygons, circles, ellipses and combinations, allowing to add color, transparency, borders and outlines, but also to include filters such as "Gaussian Blur", smoothen the image, enhance the edges etc. By means of Python scripts, based on the PIL graphic features, we created more complex structures such as smoke, fire, houses, trees, fences, gardens etc. Samples of the synthetic data for the scenarios under study are depicted in Fig. 2 (top).

Regarding the real-world datasets (used for testing the DL model), for the fire identification case, 100 aerial photos were downloaded from Google Images, 50 of them showing forest areas and another 50 showing a forest fire. For the

---

[1] Python Imaging Library. https://pypi.python.org/pypi/PIL.
[2] OpenCV. https://pypi.python.org/pypi/opencv-python.

counting houses case, 20 aerial photos from urban areas of Tanzania have been selected, from the Open AI Tanzania Challenge[3]. We cropped these photos in 100×100 pixel images, and counted the number of houses manually at each cropped photo. The result was a dataset of 60 images, each having $[0, 38]$ houses from an aerial view. Samples of the real-world datasets for the two scenarios under study are depicted in Fig. 2 (bottom). Table 2 describes the number of images used for training and testing of the two scenarios under study.

Table 2. Number of images used for training and testing of the DL models.

Scenario	Purpose	No. of images
Fire identification	Training	2,000 synthetic images
Fire identification	Testing	100 real-world aerial photos (classified as 50 images of forest and 50 images of fire)
Counting houses	Training	10,000 synthetic images (labelled with exact number of houses)
Counting houses	Testing	60 real-world aerial photos (labelled with exact number of houses)

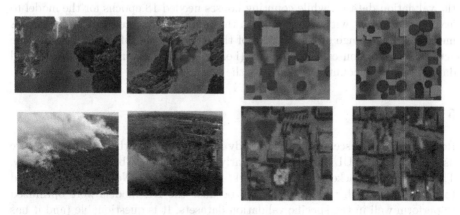

Fig. 2. Example images from the synthetic datasets (top). Example images from the real-world datasets (bottom). Images on the left are for the fire identification scenario, while images on the right for the case of the estimation of number of houses.

As a DL model, we used the Inception-v3 convolutional neural network (CNN) architecture [23] (with some adaptations, see below), as it is one of the fastest CNN architectures available, with high accuracy [2]. We used the default

---

[3] Open AI Tanzania Challenge. https://blog.werobotics.org/2018/08/06/welcome-to-the-open-ai-tanzania-challenge/.

class provided by Keras/TensorFlow during our experiments. Data augmentation was used too. For the counting houses case, our early experiments indicated we should perform adaptations to Inception-v3, to become more optimized for counting correctly. The most important design considerations were the following:

- No pre-training with other datasets (e.g. ImageNet). Filters created by ImageNet are different than the filters required for counting houses.
- Use of dropout (i.e. 35%).
- Max pooling instead of average pooling.
- Use larger filters at the convolutions at the beginning (i.e. 7×7) of the CNN.
- Use a larger value for stride (i.e. stride $= 5$).
- Use a dense layer with only one output at the end of the CNN.
- Use ReLu for the prediction of final outcome.

4   Results

Figures 3 and 4 show the results of the training of the DL models (i.e. synthetic data) and of the testing of the model in real-world data, for the fire identification and counting houses case respectively. Classification accuracy (CA) was used as the performance metric for the fire identification case, while Mean Square Error (MSE) for the counting houses scenario. The fire identification case required 24 epochs of training for the model to learn how to classify with $CA = 96\%$ on the validation dataset, while counting houses needed 18 epochs for the model to learn how to count with $MSE = 20$ on the validation dataset. In this case, MSE measures the average of the squares of the errors of the difference between the actual counts of houses in the images (i.e. ground truth counts of the real-world dataset) and the counts predicted by the DL model.

5   Discussion

Results of the two scenarios under study indicate that synthetic data can prove useful for training DL models, particularly related to UAV-based aerial imagery. This evidence is backed by related work, listed in Sect. 2. Nevertheless, we need to be cautious with these indications, because the DL models were optimized to perform well in the specific validation datasets. It is questionable (and it has not been tested) whether the DL models can produce similar results in different real-world datasets that focus on similar problems and applications [10].

The DL model for the fire identification case had very high CA. We achieved this accuracy via a hybrid approach, adding background of real forest images to the generated smoke and fire. Before this, validation CA was around 86%. On the other hand, the DL model for the counting problem still needs improvement. A $MSE = 20$ means that the model can predict the number of houses with an error of ± 4.47 houses. For example, for a photo with 20 houses, the model would predict in the range of $[16, 24]$. There is definitely space for further work on this. We note that we reached this MSE after many weeks of observations and the

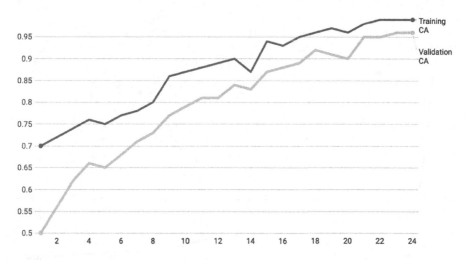

Fig. 3. Training and validation classification accuracy at the fire identification challenge.

iterative process of adding more details to the generated synthetic dataset (see Fig. 1). These details included trees, grass, swimming pools, fences etc. Each of them helped to reduce the overall error.

Applications of the proposed approach can be found in various research domains and scientific disciplines, such as agriculture, life sciences, microbiology, earth sciences etc. The approach of generative data for training DL models would be extremely useful for UAV and robotics [17,25], where computer vision is involved. It could improve operation and accuracy of automatic robots collecting crops, removing weeds or estimating yields of crops [10,18]. It could also be used in disaster monitoring and surveillance [9], where remote sensing (i.e. satellites or UAV) is used to identify events of interest (e.g. disasters, violence incidents, land cover mapping, effects on climate change etc.). Finally, it could be used in environmental studies, e.g. to understand the environmental impact of livestock agriculture [8].

Moreover, we highlight some recent state-of-art work in this domain, which relates to our proposed methodology, showing promising results in application areas other than UAV aerial imagery. First, the work in [24] incorporates two significant improvements: layered boosting (i.e. a layered approach, where training is done in stages) and selective sampling (i.e. streamline the training process by reducing the impact of the low quality samples, such as trivial cases or outliers). Second, the concept of Structured Domain Randomization (SDR) places objects and distractors randomly according to probability distributions [16] and from probabilistic scene grammars [11], which arise from the specific problem at hand. In this manner, SDR-generated imagery enables the neural network to take the context around an object into consideration during detection. Third, related specifically to counting, the work in [13] evades the hard task of learning

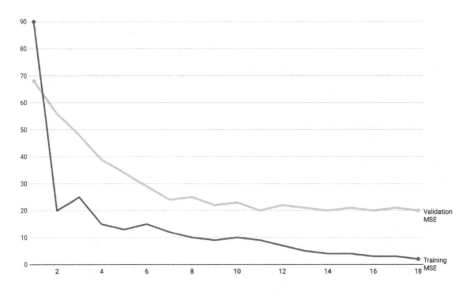

Fig. 4. Training and validation MSE at the counting houses challenge.

to detect and localize individual object instances. Instead, it casts the problem as that of estimating an image density whose integral over any image region gives the count of objects within that region. Furthermore, our work, as well as the aforementioned promising approaches [13,16,24] can be combined with Generative Adversarial Networks (GANs), to stylize synthetic images to look more like those captured in the real world [14,26].

Finally, we note another recent possibility, that of utilizing the *Aerial Informatics and Robotics* platform [22] for generating seamlessly training data related to UAV-based aerial imagery. This platform acts as an easy-to-use simulator that aims to enable designers and developers of robotic systems to generate graphical data. Its biggest advantage is that it uses recent advances in computation and graphics to simulate the physics and perception such that the environment realistically reflects the actual world.

6   Conclusion

This paper has described preliminary work in the approach of generating synthetic training data for facilitating the learning procedure of DL models, with a focus on UAV-based aerial imagery. The general methodology of this approach was described, and preliminary results were presented, focused on two different challenges: a classification problem of fire identification in forests as well as a counting problem of estimating number of houses in urban areas. Results were promising, but there is still space for improvement, especially in the counting houses case. Use of synthetic data for training DL models in aerial imagery is a new exciting possibility for the research community working in this area, especially in cases where ground-truth data is scarce or expensive to produce.

For future work, we aim to experiment with more realistic generation of synthetic data, by using game engines such as the Unity development platform[4]. We also aim to apply our methodology in new UAV-related applications such as human crowd counting, identification and counting of endangered species and wild animals etc., enhancing our methodology with the new proposals described in Sect. 5, in order to minimize the distribution gap between the rendered outputs of the synthetic data and the target real-world data.

References

1. Amara, J., Bouaziz, B., Algergawy, A., et al.: A deep learning-based approach for banana leaf diseases classification. In: BTW (Workshops), pp. 79–88 (2017)
2. Canziani, A., Paszke, A., Culurciello, E.: An analysis of deep neural network models for practical applications. arXiv preprint arXiv:1605.07678 (2016)
3. Douarre, C., Schielein, R., Frindel, C., Gerth, S., Rousseau, D.: Deep learning based root-soil segmentation from x-ray tomography. bioRxiv, p. 071662 (2016)
4. Dyrmann, M., Mortensen, A.K., Midtiby, H.S., Jorgensen, R.N., et al.: Pixel-wise classification of weeds and crops in images by using a fully convolutional neural network. In: Proceedings of the International Conference on Agricultural Engineering, Aarhus, Denmark, pp. 26–29 (2016)
5. Gaidon, A., Wang, Q., Cabon, Y., Vig, E.: Virtual worlds as proxy for multi-object tracking analysis. In: Proceedings of the IEEE Conference on Computer Vision and Pattern Recognition, pp. 4340–4349 (2016)
6. Goodfellow, I., et al.: Generative adversarial nets. In: Advances in Neural Information Processing Systems, pp. 2672–2680 (2014)
7. Kamilaris, A.: Simulating training data for deep learning models. In: Machine Learning in the Environmental Sciences Workshop, in Proceedings of EnviroInfo 2018, Munich, Germany, September 2018
8. Kamilaris, A., Assumpcio, A., Blasi, A.B., Torrellas, M., Prenafeta-Boldú, F.X.: Estimating the environmental impact of agriculture by means of geospatial and big data analysis: the case of catalonia. In: Otjacques, B., Hitzelberger, P., Naumann, S., Wohlgemuth, V. (eds.) From Science to Society. PI, pp. 39–48. Springer, Cham (2018). https://doi.org/10.1007/978-3-319-65687-8_4
9. Kamilaris, A., Prenafeta-Boldu, F.X.: Disaster monitoring using unmanned aerial vehicles and deep learning. In: Disaster Management for Resilience and Public Safety Workshop, in Proceedings of EnviroInfo 2017, Luxembourg, September 2017
10. Kamilaris, A., Prenafeta-Boldu, F.X.: Deep learning in agriculture: a survey. Comput. Electron. Agric. **147**, 70–90 (2018)
11. Kar, A., et al.: Meta-sim: learning to generate synthetic datasets. arXiv preprint arXiv:1904.11621 (2019)
12. Lehmussola, A., Ruusuvuori, P., Selinummi, J., Huttunen, H., Yli-Harja, O.: Computational framework for simulating fluorescence microscope images with cell populations. IEEE Trans. Med. Imaging **26**(7), 1010–1016 (2007)
13. Lempitsky, V., Zisserman, A.: Learning to count objects in images. In: Advances in Neural Information Processing Systems, pp. 1324–1332 (2010)
14. Li, P., Liang, X., Jia, D., Xing, E.P.: Semantic-aware grad-GAN for virtual-to-real urban scene adaption. arXiv preprint arXiv:1801.01726 (2018)

---

[4] Unity. https://unity.com.

15. Olah, C., et al.: The building blocks of interpretability. Distill **3**(3), e10 (2018)
16. Prakash, A., et al.: Structured domain randomization: Bridging the reality gap by context-aware synthetic data. arXiv preprint arXiv:1810.10093 (2018)
17. Puig, X., et al.: Virtualhome: simulating household activities via programs. In: Proceedings of the IEEE Conference on Computer Vision and Pattern Recognition, pp. 8494–8502 (2018)
18. Rahnemoonfar, M., Sheppard, C.: Deep count: fruit counting based on deep simulated learning. Sensors **17**(4), 905 (2017)
19. Richter, S.R., Vineet, V., Roth, S., Koltun, V.: Playing for data: ground truth from computer games. In: Leibe, B., Matas, J., Sebe, N., Welling, M. (eds.) ECCV 2016. LNCS, vol. 9906, pp. 102–118. Springer, Cham (2016). https://doi.org/10.1007/978-3-319-46475-6_7
20. Ros, G., Sellart, L., Materzynska, J., Vazquez, D., Lopez, A.M.: The synthia dataset: a large collection of synthetic images for semantic segmentation of urban scenes. In: Proceedings of the IEEE Conference on Computer Vision and Pattern Recognition, pp. 3234–3243 (2016)
21. Schmidhuber, J.: Deep learning in neural networks: an overview. Neural Netw. **61**, 85–117 (2015)
22. Shah, S., Dey, D., Lovett, C., Kapoor, A.: Aerial Informatics and Robotics Platform. Microsoft Research, Washigton (2017)
23. Szegedy, C., Vanhoucke, V., Ioffe, S., Shlens, J., Wojna, Z.: Rethinking the inception architecture for computer vision. In: Proceedings of the IEEE Conference on Computer Vision and Pattern Recognition, pp. 2818–2826 (2016)
24. Walach, E., Wolf, L.: Learning to count with CNN boosting. In: Leibe, B., Matas, J., Sebe, N., Welling, M. (eds.) ECCV 2016. LNCS, vol. 9906, pp. 660–676. Springer, Cham (2016). https://doi.org/10.1007/978-3-319-46475-6_41
25. Wu, Y., Wu, Y., Gkioxari, G., Tian, Y.: Building generalizable agents with a realistic and rich 3D environment. arXiv preprint arXiv:1801.02209 (2018)
26. Zhu, J.Y., Park, T., Isola, P., Efros, A.A.: Unpaired image-to-image translation using cycle-consistent adversarial networks. In: Proceedings of the IEEE International Conference on Computer Vision, pp. 2223–2232 (2017)

Computer Vision and Deep Learning-Enabled UAVs: Proposed Use Cases for Visually Impaired People in a Smart City

Moustafa M. Nasralla[1(✉)], Ikram U. Rehman[2], Drishty Sobnath[3], and Sara Paiva[4]

[1] Department of Communications and Networks Engineering,
Prince Sultan University, Riyadh, Saudi Arabia
`mnasralla@psu.edu.sa`
[2] School of Computing and Engineering, University of West London, London, UK
`ikram.rehman@uwl.ac.uk`
[3] Research, Innovation and Enterprise, Solent University, Southampton, UK
`drishty.sobnath@solent.ac.uk`
[4] ARC4DigiT, Instituto Politécnico de Viana do Castelo, Viana do Castelo, Portugal
`sara.paiva@estg.ipvc.pt`

Abstract. Technological research and innovation have advanced at a rapid pace in recent years, and one group hoping to benefit from this, is visually impaired people (VIP). Technology may enable them to find new ways of travelling around smart cities, thus improving their quality of life (QoL). Currently, there are approximately 110 million VIP worldwide, and continuous research is crucial to find innovative solutions to their mobility problems. Recent advances such as the increase in Unmanned Aerial Vehicles (UAVs), smartphones and wearable devices, together with an ever-growing uptake of deep learning, computer vision, the Internet of Things (IoT), and virtual and augmented reality (VR)/(AR), have provided VIP with the hope of having an improved QoL. In particular, indoor and outdoor spaces could be improved with the use of such technologies to make them suitable for VIP. This paper examines use cases both indoors and outdoors and provides recommendations of how deep learning and computer vision-enabled UAVs could be employed in smart cities to improve the QoL for VIP in the coming years.

Keywords: Deep learning · Computer vision · UAVs · Drone · Visually impaired people (VIP) · Smart city

1 Introduction

According to the authors in [1], the World Health Organization (WHO) categorises visual function under four headings: normal and moderate vision, vision impairment and blindness. Globally, it is estimated that there are 38 million blind

© Springer Nature Switzerland AG 2019
M. Vento and G. Percannella (Eds.): CAIP 2019 Workshops, CCIS 1089, pp. 91–99, 2019.
https://doi.org/10.1007/978-3-030-29930-9_9

people and 110 million people with visual disabilities. The aims of research in this area, according to [2], have centred on finding solutions to enhance the quality of life (QoL) of those afflicted, particularly in terms of safe mobility in urban areas, and enabling them to undertake daily tasks safely. In recent years there have been substantial technological developments that could potentially improve the QoL of the visually impaired. This is particularly evident in the advancement of navigation within smart cities, which has greatly encouraged visually impaired people (VIP) [2]. The authors in [3] identify the expression 'smart city' as a term originating in the 1990s that encompasses the evolution of city development, technological advancement, exponential modernisation and globalisation. Poor eyesight should not preclude people from taking an active part in everyday life. The current pace of life necessitates tasks involving an increasingly complex input of information. In particular, education and employment require access to a wide range of detailed information. Visually impaired people in smart cities, according to [4], benefit from the wide-ranging support provided by a profusion of innovations: cloud computing, embedded systems, remote sensors, wireless networks and robotics, sophisticated smartphones, UAVs, the Internet of Things (IoT), augmented and virtual reality (AR/VR) and artificial intelligence (AI). UAVs [2], sometimes referred as drones, are a class of aircrafts that can fly without the onboard presence of pilots, which could also provide potential solutions for the mobility of VIP. It is the nascent time for smart cities, like those now developing in New York, Beijing, Singapore and Dubai. Smart cities of the future will expand and develop to incorporate new technology and ideas that will be tested and subsequently incorporated into their infrastructure. This bodes well for VIP, improving their QoL and if the current investment is sustained, this will lead towards full incorporation into the experience. The European Innovation Partnership on Small Cities and Communities (EIP-SCC) is an initiative partly funded by a one-billion-euro investment from the European Commission. The aim of the partnership, according to the European Commission in [5], is to unite citizens and industry in more than 300 cities. The visually impaired will be one group that gains advantage from this project. The authors in [6] observe that technology is advancing to the extent that with IoT-enabled wireless development, the increased usage of UAVs and the employment of big data analysis and AI, image recognition and the achievement of certain activities are within the realms of possibility. Innovative recommendations include the employment of UAVs, utilising their inbuilt navigation systems to replace the established guide dog and assist VIP with their mobility, guiding them to their objective (Fig. 1). Drones or UAVs have the added benefits of image analysis and recognition. A built-in camera is able to identify likely hazards, and via either audio signals, messages or by vibratory sensors, can warn VIP of potential threats in their path. Furthermore, the provision of a collision detection system in intelligent drones would alert a VIP of any threat of contact with people or objects [7].

This paper makes recommendations referring to the development of technologies to meet these requirements. The aim is to provide VIP with the timely enhancement of movement and activity in a smart city environment. The rest of the paper is organised as follows. Section 2 provides background of deep learning

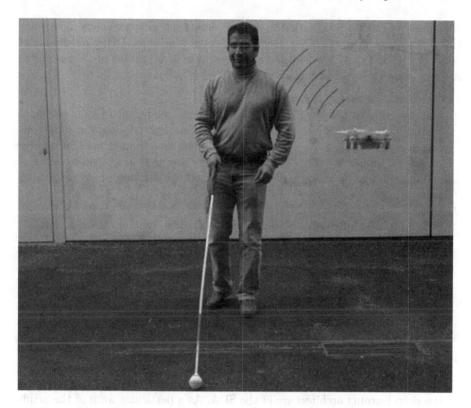

Fig. 1. VIP receiving drone-provided navigation guidance [7].

and computer vision application. Section 3 provides related work. In Sect. 4, we present deep learning and computer vision-enabled UAV use cases to assist VIP. Finally, Sect. 5 concludes the paper.

2   Deep Learning and Computer Vision Applications

Deep learning belongs to the family of machine learning algorithms, which is best-suited to build complex concepts out of simpler ones. Its learning process typically involves several hierarchical levels as opposed to other machine learning techniques (e.g. Neural Networks) [8]. In recent times, deep learning has become a hot topic of research and its application in the field of computer vision (e.g. object and image analysis and recognition etc.) has shown phenomenal results. Furthermore, computational models of multiple processing layers, utilising deep learning, are able to learn and reproduce data with multiple layers of abstraction, emulating the perception and comprehension of multimodal information as processed by the brain, thereby assimilating complex structures of large-scale data [8]. Deep learning has enabled major advancements in solving a number of computer vision problems: face and action recognition, object detection, motion tracking and human pose estimation, and semantic segmentation [8]. Convolutional neural networks (CNNs), Deep Boltzmann Machines (DBMs), deep belief networks (DBNs) and stacked denoising autoencoders (SDAs) are some of the most prominent deep learning skills, described as follows:

1. Convolutional Neural Networks
   The structure of the visual system led to the development of Convolutional Neural Networks (CNNs), made up of convolutional, pooling and fully connected main types of layers. This highly effective system is used in diverse computer applications, where multiple layers are used in an end-to-end format [9], and it provides one of the most effective forms of deep learning applications.
2. Deep Belief Networks and Deep Boltzmann Machines
   First proposed by Hinton et al., the Restricted Boltzmann Machine (RBM) is a Generative Stochastic Network (GSN) framework. Both the DBM and the DBN are part of the 'Boltzmann family', deep learning models that use the RBM as a learning module [10]. Based on the RBM, the machine is constrained, in that both the visible and hidden units need to form a part of the bipartite graph. This enables efficient training algorithms, especially gradient-based contrastive divergence algorithms [8].
3. Stacked Denoising Autoencoders
   RBMs are a major component of DBNs; SDAs are built around the autoencoder as the principal component. On this basis, it is necessary to describe the basic features of the autoencoder and its denoising model, prior to explaining the deep learning architecture of the SDA. As a particular form of the artificial neural network, the autoencoder is employed to learn efficient encodings. Rather than present given inputs to the network in order to previse a specific target value, the autoencoder is programmed to create its own inputs, whereby the output and input vectors have the same ambit [11].

In a smart city scenario, where independent mobility for people with functional disabilities and in particular VIP is regarded as one of the primary objectives, the aforementioned deep learning methodologies could provide significant improvements in their everyday routine. For instance, CNNs could be used for path learning, indoor and outdoor navigation, as well as localisation. This will require a GPS device embedded inside the UAVs, leading towards independent mobility of the VIP within urban areas. Whereas, DBNs and SDNs can be jointly used in a single framework for feature extraction and object/image recognition. Moreover, the latter methods can be envisioned as suitable candidates for obstacle avoidance both in indoors and outdoors use cases, which are discussed in details in Sect. 4. It is worth mentioning that the success in imitating human perception of the aforementioned deep learning-based UAVs depends on the rigorousness of its training and learning phases. The more rigorously the learning model is trained, the higher the navigation and recognition accuracy. Deep learning will help those with disabilities, particularly VIP. The crucial benefit is to have real-time support. To achieve this, drones or UAVs need to have systems installed for maximum deep learning benefits. Outside real-time support will not necessarily fulfil the need for access to be unrestricted by time or location. The IoT and similar advances in technology would provide backend information and data. However, the drone is the front-end provider, delivering essential and timely information to VIP during their daily activities. Recently, research, academic and industrial entities have more widely adopted AI and deep learning-enabled intelligent computer vision systems, cooperating to improve the QoL of VIP. The emphasis has been on developing more advanced navigation and hazard avoidance systems, utilising AI-based solutions. The requirements have encompassed such diverse subjects as navigation tools to traverse indoor and outdoor areas, computer vision, AR/VR tools to enhance human vision, road crossing assistance, the location and identification of bus stops and drone guidance. This has been made possible by advancements in image and object capturing systems, and AI and machine learning development techniques such as deep learning, fuzzy inference systems (FISs) and neural networks.

3 Related Work

There is the prospect of major development for the mobility of VIP in a smart city environment. Deep-learning-based UAVs and the advancement of computer vision are evolving and being enhanced constantly to improve hazard detection. Currently, information and communication applications (ICTs) are being employed for the improvement of QoL for VIP. The recently completed Ambient Assisted Living (AAL) project was an initiative encompassing a number of EU projects with this aim. There are three stages in drone image recognition, namely (1) object detection and capture, (2) segmentation, and (3) object recognition. Deep neural networks (DNNs) are used increasingly for object recognition, replacing previous machine learning algorithms such as support vector machines (SVMs) and neural networks. The DNN system works on a deep-learning form of machine learning technique and is proving to be adaptable in incorporating environmental changes and identifying minor changes in an extracted object feature [12]. Current and predicted development results identify image recognition-based drones as paramount in improving the QoL of VIP in a smart city environment. However, there is a need for a large dataset for DNN training, which is one the challenges in implementing such systems. This places a resultant high demand on time and computer power resources, requirements that can seriously curtail drone battery life. The methods used for image-based object detection have proved efficient, particularly in an agricultural setting, where techniques employing classical shape and colour-based ground vehicle detection have proved to be effective [13]. The development of CNNs [8] has enabled the resolving of object detection issues, based on the deep learning method. In the ImageNet competition, algorithms like Single Shot Detector (SSD) and You Only Look Once (YOLO) [14] performed well in the detection phase, while AlexNet and GoogLeNet displayed excellent performance and speed results. Nevertheless, the algorithms lacked the computing power requirement needed for an embedded system. As an alternative, a drone-based prototype navigation system was presented, incorporating an en-route auditory information and warning system for VIP travelling to their objective [7]. It was recommended that VIP wear a device such as a bracelet to facilitate the passage of voice directions from the VIP to the drone. Five walking trials were conducted, using a blind VIP as a case study. Various movements were tested such as making full 180-degree turns, walking in a straight line and navigating through a crowded room. The drone gave a clearly audible signal to warn both the VIP and people nearby of its presence. The trials proved successful, which pleased the VIP, although neither deep learning nor object recognition was tested, as the aim of the trial was to evaluate the navigation capabilities of the system. In addition, during the trial, the VIP used his white cane to locate nearby obstacles. Studies investigating methods to improve the QoL of VIP [15–20] recorded a range of aids used to assist in avoiding hazards; these included microcontrollers, webcams, audio feedback mechanisms and ultrasonic sensors. The limitations of mobility and costs were taken into consideration, particularly as the equipment tended to be in the form of cumbersome prototypes with neither deep learning nor AI in their tactile vision systems.

4   Use Cases

A set of use cases was presented to highlight the requirement for the employment of drones incorporating AI and deep learning, to enhance QoL. The aim was to establish safe and effective movement indoor and outdoor using VIP as subjects. Every case presented evidence of the advantages of intelligent drone usage.

4.1   Indoor Scenario

It is possible to configure drones to operate indoors, employing a deep-learning form of machine-learning mechanism. For safe and effective navigation, a number of features need to be provisioned:

1. The drones need to be programmed to navigate the indoor paths available.
2. Real-time images of the environment to be used by the VIP should be installed into the drone built-in camera.
3. Accurate information about en-route hazards should be available from image and object recognition mechanisms.
4. Drones should be fitted with collision detection IoT-based sensors to protect against hitting people or structures.

Navigation is not the only service intelligent drones are able to provide for VIP. Reference images of misplaced or lost items can be uploaded via the computer vision and image analysis mechanisms. Once the drone has identified and located the item and established its coordinates it can guide the user to its position. Sensors linked to the guide drones with their sensor-based surveillance systems could monitor VIP health states, particularly in emergency situations such as falling or sudden illness. Sensors, either worn by VIP or sited in smart homes, would be able to ascertain whether the subject had suffered a fall or was generally experiencing movement difficulties. Microsoft Kinect, an example of a drone-mounted motion sensor, is able to identify certain tasks being carried out by VIP. In a study, the authors in [21] observe that the system is also able to identify faces and objects, which further assists in reducing the possibility of indoor accidents. Google Home and Amazon Echo Dot are drone-installed voice activation programmes allowing access to a range of services such as news and weather, music and audiobooks.

4.2 Outdoor Scenario

The prime concern for the safety of VIP and the elderly is mobility related, to allow the negotiation of both familiar and unfamiliar hazardous areas. Drones, according to the authors in [4], can assist in navigating VIP safely in smart city open areas, by providing:

1. Signal-based alerts, audible and vibrotactile, to provide pedestrians with accurate positioning information.
2. Shopping support using a mobile product recognition system.
3. Adapted mobile-assisted city apps for VIP use.

The mobility of VIP can be identified and aided by the employment of deep learning and computer vision. The systems can be developed further, recording known VIP routes, particularly in smart cities where the network infrastructure is developed, and UAVs can be used effectively, and when combined with voice instruction functions can effectively direct people to their nominated destination. An added benefit is in tourist areas, where the systems are able to describe the local setting through which the person is passing, thereby expanding user cognisance of their location. Guidance for university and college VIP students greatly enhances their experience. Drones assist them in moving unaided from lecture to lecture around the campus, increasing their safety and reducing possible anxiety, thereby improving their QoL in the learning environment. The computer-based algorithms help provide information and direction to places of interest such as libraries, lecture halls and cafes. They can be programmed to provide real-time information on possible problem areas, such as busy thoroughfares and traffic crossings, all of which can be accessed and questioned audibly by the VIP. The aim is to establish a personalised VIP/system relationship. The authors in [22] observe that transportation is a major issue for VIP at every level; local, regional, national and international. Within smart cities, drones are able to provide detailed assistance, locating bus stops, and audibly giving route details together with departure and arrival times, and recognising the right bus for the user. This greatly benefits VIP, enabling them to travel on public transport without having to ask for assistance. Supermarket shopping is a task where drones can greatly assist VIP. Those UAVs equipped with systems such as OS X developed by Apple, which has VoiceOver features, use deep learning-based image recognition technologies, and are able to identify products and make comparisons. Audible instructions and information programmes need to be user friendly in order to allow VIP to operate mobile phone apps easily.

5   Conclusion

Indoors, VIP need to be able to move without colliding with obstacles or objects and also be able to locate specific items. Outdoors, the system should assist them in safe passage, identifying the best routes and crossing points, in addition to giving audible transport information, bus stops, timings and bus identification. Smart cities have the functionality to improve the QoL of VIP. Their development, together with technological advancements, lead to the goal of allowing the visually impaired to take an active part in social events and provides them with a greater degree of independence. The exponential development of technological advances promises greater freedom for VIP, not only in safer and freer movement but also the benefit of a better QoL. Smart cities are modelled to allow the straightforward integration and management of ICT-based technology. Computer vision and deep learning functions, together with sensing and monitoring capabilities, are integrated to exploit current and future evolution. The aim of this paper is to identify the development of computer vision and deep learning-enabled drones, and the need for obstacle and collision detection systems combined with image recognition features to be integrated into a single unit. The driving force has been to enhance the safety and QoL of VIP in smart cities, identifying use cases for both indoor and outdoor movement. There is an ongoing need to develop the capabilities and efficiency of deep learning and computer vision-enabled drones, particularly in smart cities.

Acknowledgement. Dr. Moustafa Nasralla would like to acknowledge the Department of Communications and Networks Engineering at Prince Sultan University (PSU) for the valued support and research environmental provision which have led to completing this work. Dr. Ikram Ur Rehman would like to thank the School of Computing and Engineering, University of West London for its support and research provision. Dr. Drishty Sobnath would like to thank the Research Innovation and Enterprise department at Solent University for its continuous support that led to the completion of this study. Dr. Sara Paiva would like to thank the Instituto Politécnico de Viana do Castelo for its continuous support that led to the completion of this study.

References

1. Texeira, C., Toledo, A.S., da Silva Amorim, A., Kofuji, S.T., Rogério dos Santos, V.: Visual impairment and smart cities: perspectives on mobility. JOJ Ophthalmol. **3** (2017)
2. Ramadhan, A.J.: Wearable smart system for visually impaired people. Sensors **13**(3), 834 (2018)
3. Gibson, D.V., Kozmetsky, G., Smilor, R.W.: The Technopolis Phenomenon: Smart Cities, Fast Systems, Global Networks. Rowman & Littlefield Publishers, Lanham (1992)
4. Skouby, K.E., Kivimäki, A., Haukipuro, L., Lynggaard, P., Windekilde, I.: Smart cities and the ageing population. In: 32nd Meeting of WWRF, Marrakech, Morocco. https://pdfs.semanticscholar.org/d7a5/84f867996dbdf78a34697523c537dae218bc.pdf
5. European Commission: General Assembly of the European Innovation Partnership on Smart Cities and Communities (EIP-SCC) — European Commission (2018)

6. Philip, N.Y., Rehman, I.U.: Towards 5G health for medical video streaming over small cells. In: Kyriacou, E., Christofides, S., Pattichis, C. (eds.) XIV Mediterranean Conference on Medical and Biological Engineering and Computing 2016. IFMBE Proceedings, vol. 57. Springer, Cham (2016). https://doi.org/10.1007/978-3-319-32703-7_215

7. Avila, M., Funk, M., Henze, N.: DroneNavigator: using drones for navigating visually impaired persons. In: Proceedings of the 17th International ACM SIGACCESS Conference on Computers & Accessibility, pp. 327–328 (2015)

8. Voulodimos, A., Doulamis, N., Doulamis, A., Protopapadakis, E.: Deep learning for computer vision: a brief review. Comput. Intell. Neurosci. Article ID 7068349 (2018). https://doi.org/10.1155/2018/7068349

9. Liang, M., Hu, X.: Recurrent convolutional neural network for object recognition. In: Proceedings of the IEEE Conference on Computer Vision and Pattern Recognition, pp. 3367–3375 (2015)

10. Hinton, G.E., Sejnowski, T.J.: Learning and relearning in Boltzmann machines. In: Parallel Distributed Processing: Explorations in the Microstructure of Cognition, pp. 282–317 (1986)

11. Baltrušaitis, T., Ahuja, C., Morency, L.P.: Multimodal machine learning: a survey and taxonomy. IEEE Trans. Pattern Anal. Mach. Intell. **41**(2), 423–443 (2018)

12. Carrio, A., Sampedro, C., Rodriguez-Ramos, A., Campoy, P.: A review of deep learning methods and applications for unmanned aerial vehicles. J. Sens. **2017**, Article ID 3296874, 13 p. (2017). https://doi.org/10.1155/2017/3296874

13. Hung, C., Xu, Z., Sukkarieh, S.: Feature learning based approach for weed classification using high resolution aerial images from a digital camera mounted on a UAV. Remote Sens. **6**(12), 12037–12054 (2014)

14. Jung, S., Hwang, S., Shin, H., Shim, D.H.: Perception, guidance, and navigation for indoor autonomous drone racing using deep learning. IEEE Robot. Autom. Lett. **3**(3), 2539–2544 (2018)

15. Cardin, S., Thalmann, D., Vexo, F.: A wearable system for mobility improvement of visually impaired people. Vis. Comput. **23**(2), 109–118 (2007)

16. Dunai, L.D., Lengua, I.L., Tortajada, I., Simon, F.B.: Obstacle detectors for visually impaired people. In: 2014 International Conference on Optimization of Electrical and Electronic Equipment, OPTIM (2014)

17. Gharani, P., Karimi, H.A.: Context-aware obstacle detection for navigation by visually impaired. Image Vis. Comput. **64**, 103–115 (2017)

18. Jonnalagedda, A., et al.: Enhancing the Safety of Visually Impaired Travelers in and around Transit Stations (2014)

19. Lee, C.L., Chen, C.Y., Sung, P.C., Lu, S.Y.: Assessment of a simple obstacle detection device for the visually impaired. Appl. Ergon. **45**(4), 817–824 (2014)

20. Poggi, M., Mattoccia, S.: A wearable mobility aid for the visually impaired based on embedded 3D vision and deep learning. In: Proceedings - IEEE Symposium on Computers and Communications (2016)

21. Rahman, M.M., Poon, B., Amin, M.A., Yan, H.: Support system using microsoft kinect and mobile phone for daily activity of visually impaired. In: Yang, G.-C., Ao, S.-I., Huang, X., Castillo, O. (eds.) Transactions on Engineering Technologies, pp. 425–440. Springer, Dordrecht (2015). https://doi.org/10.1007/978-94-017-9588-3_32

22. Patricio, M., Haidee, L., Ciro, L., Telma, R., Felipe, F.: Analysis and proposed improvements in the support for the visually impaired in the use of public transportation. In: SMART 2015: The Fourth International Conference on Smart Systems, Devices and Technologies (2015). ISBN 978-1-61208-414-5

UAV Image Based Crop and Weed Distribution Estimation on Embedded GPU Boards

Mulham Fawakherji[1], Ciro Potena[1], Domenico D. Bloisi[2(✉)], Marco Imperoli[1], Alberto Pretto[3], and Daniele Nardi[1]

[1] Departmemt of Computer, Control and Management Engineering,
Sapienza University of Rome, via Ariosto 25, 00184 Rome, Italy
nardi@diag.uniroma1.it
[2] Departmemt of Mathematics, Computer Science, and Economics,
University of Basilicata, viale dell'Ateneo Lucano, 10, 85100 Potenza, Italy
domenico.bloisi@unibas.it
[3] IT+Robotics Srl, Padova, Italy
alberto.pretto@it-robotics.it

Abstract. The use of unmanned aerial vehicles (UAVs) in precision agriculture is gaining more and more interest. In this paper, we present a deep learning based method for estimating the crop and weed distribution from images captured by a UAV. The proposed approach runs on an embedded board equipped with a GPU. Quantitative experimental results have been obtained using real images from two different public datasets. The results demonstrate the effectiveness of the proposed approach.

Keywords: Crop/weed distribution estimation ·
Crop/weed detection · Precision agriculture

1 Introduction

Sustainable agriculture requires the implementation of intelligent strategies for weed control in order to minimize the usage of chemical inputs. In traditional weed control, the agro-chemical inputs are uniformly applied to the field. Although this practice is simple and effective, it can lead to a higher usage of chemical inputs than the required one. Building a representation of the field status (e.g., the spacial distribution of crop and weeds) offers the potential to drastically reduce the amount of treatments applied to the field. Unmanned aerial vehicles (UAVs) can be used to address this task. UAVs have become suitable platforms thanks to their low cost and their capability to cover large areas in a short amount of time. Moreover, conversely from ground vehicles, UAVs do not impact the field. However, they can carry a limited amount of payload and the flight autonomy is still low (typically, less than 1 h).

ⓒ Springer Nature Switzerland AG 2019
M. Vento and G. Percannella (Eds.): CAIP 2019 Workshops, CCIS 1089, pp. 100–108, 2019.
https://doi.org/10.1007/978-3-030-29930-9_10

Fig. 1. Left: AscTec Neo multirotor. Right: Jetson TX2 board.

In this paper, we analyze UAV images to infer the status of the field in terms of crop and weed distribution using a power-efficient, embedded GPU board. Our method takes as input multi-spectral images and performs crop/weeds segmentation to estimate their distribution. The segmentation process is based on an encoder-decoder architecture for pixel-wise segmentation and it allows to distinguish between plants that might be slightly different or even partially overlapping. In particular, the architecture is based on the UNet network [12] with a modified VGG-16 encoder. To estimate the weed distribution, we perform a further post-processing step that, starting from the segmented image, divides it into a fixed size grid and then computes for each cell the crop/weeds statistics (e.g., weed distribution and segmentation confidence).

A quantitative experimental evaluation has been carried on real-data coming from two datasets acquired by UAVs. The first dataset [13] is publicly available and it is made of 155 images about sugar beets. The second dataset contains images acquired with an AscTec Neo multirotor (see the left side of Fig. 1) in a corn field and we manually annotated 75 images. The proposed algorithm has been tested on a Jetson TX2 board (see the right side of Fig. 1) using three channels in input (NIR, RED, and NDVI). The obtained mean accuracy was 95% and for vegetation detection (e.g., pixel classification into soil and plants classes only) we achieved 99% using NDVI index as input.

2 Related Work

The problem of estimating the crop/weeds distribution in farm lands has been addressed by either employing handcrafted features (e.g., [8,9]) or end-to-end methods (e.g., [3,11,14]). Early work in crop/weeds classification used features extracted by co-occurrence matrices (CM) from hue, saturation, and intensity color space [15], morphological and color features as input of a Fuzzy [6], or CM texture statistics as input variables for a back propagation neural network [2]. More recently, Random Forest (RF) classifiers have been used to deal with the problem. Haug *et al.* [5] propose to use a large number of simple features extracted from an overlapping neighborhood around sparse pixel positions, while in [8] the authors extended the method by adding a relative plant arrangement prior and a further Markov Random Field (MRF) based optimization to exploit the topological relationships between keypoints. The latter has been further extended in [9] by adapting the features to be used on UAVs and by handling RGB images without requiring near-infrared (NIR) data.

To overcome the inflexibility and limitations in terms of expressiveness of handcrafted vision pipelines, crop/weeds distribution estimation systems moved toward an end-to-end approach based on Convolutional Neural Networks (CNNs). Potena *et al.* [11] use a cascade of CNNs for crop-weed classification, where the first network detects vegetation and then vegetation pixels only are further classified by a deeper crop/weed CNN. In our previous work [4], we propose a similar architecture by focusing on overcoming the generalization limitations of CNNs when a few pixel-wise annotated data is available. Specifically, the first network performs a robust binary segmentation between vegetation and soil terrain, while the second one runs a blob-wise classification. SegNet [1] architecture has been also exploited to perform crop/weeds classification. In [3] the authors focus on reducing the labelling burden by using synthetic realistic images, while in [14] the authors propose to use the SegNet architecture for multispectral crop/weed classification from a UAV. Similarly, Lottes *et al.* [7] propose an encoder-decoder network structure that also incorporates spatial information by considering image sequences. The results show how the additional data aid the system in generalizing to previously unseen fields under varying environmental conditions. Milioto *et al.* [10] use a similar architecture by combining RGB images with additional input channels that incorporate vegetation indexes.

3   Methods

Our goal is to process images taken by a UAV to extract high-level information about the field, like weed and crop density, instead of finding the exact location for weed inside the images. The high-level information can be sent to a ground robot to perform selective spraying. To achieve our goal, first we train a CNN to build a model able to detect crop and weed in the images, then we compute the distribution of the weed and the crop with a confidence based on the output of the trained model. The flowchart in Fig. 2 shows the main steps of the proposed method.

Crop/Weed Segmentation. To perform pixel-wise segmentation of the input image into 3 classes (i.e., weed, crop, and soil), we use a modified version of

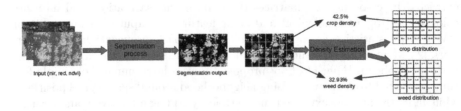

Fig. 2. Flowchart of the proposed approach.

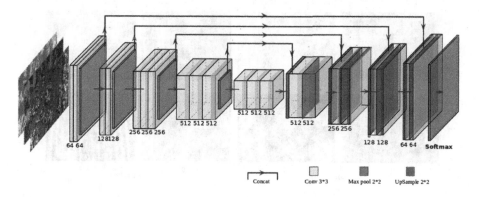

Fig. 3. The architecture of the image segmentation network.

the UNet semantic segmentation network [12], which is made of a contracting encoder along with a symmetric expanding decoder. In our implementation, the contracting path consists of a VGG-16 structure modified by removing the last fully connected layers and fine-tuning the other layers.

The segmentation network is designed with a contracting path composed of 4 blocks: The first and second composed of 2-convolutional layers, the third and fourth composed of 3-convolutional layers. We used a 3×3 fixed size filter and ReLu activation function, each block followed by max-pooling layer. The expanding path is designed with 4-convolutional layers, where each layer is composed of a batch normalization, 4-upsampling layers and a soft-max pixel-wise classifier.

The scheme of the segmentation network is shown in Fig. 3. Between the contracting and expanding paths, there is a bottleneck consisting of three convolutional layers combined with batch normalization and a dropout activation function. The indices of spatial information in the pooling operations are spread through the expansive path, which contains a sequence of up-convolution operations of features encoded in the contracting path.

Crop/Weed Distribution Estimation. The second main step in our pipeline (see Fig. 2) concerns the computation of the distribution of weed and crop inside the image. In this stage, the mask generated during the segmentation process is divided using a fixed size grid (28 cells) based on the segmentation output size. Then, we compute for each cell the crop/weeds statistics (e.g., weed distribution and segmentation confidence). The distribution for a specific class in each cell is obtained by computing the number of pixels of that class inside the cell (Kc) divided by the total number of pixel inside the cell (see Eq. 1).

$$D_c = \frac{K_c}{\sum_{i=1}^{n} K_i} \tag{1}$$

where D_c represent the distribution of class c, n is the number of classes, and K_c is the total number of pixels belonging to class c inside the cell. For each cell, we also compute a per-class confidence $MCon_c$ as the average of the class

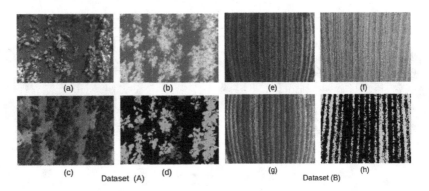

Fig. 4. Image samples from the datasets used in our experiments. (a), (b), (c), and (d) represent NIR, NDVI, RED, and ground truth from sugar beet dataset. (e), (f), (g), and (h) represent NIR, RGB, RED, and ground truth from corn dataset.

probabilities $P(\cdot)$ provided by the network of Fig. 3 for all the cell pixels X_i that are classified with class c, i.e.:

$$MCon_c = \frac{\sum_{i=1}^{K_c} P(X_i = c)}{K_c} \tag{2}$$

4   Experimental Results

The experiments aim at measuring

1. the performance of VGG-UNet architecture on the Jetson TX2 board, which can easily be installed on a small UAV.
2. the accuracy of the segmentation network to classify the image pixels into three classes, namely soil, crop, and weed with varying input data.
3. the performance of the segmentation network on background removal (e.g., pixel classification into only two classes soil and plants) also with varying input data.

Dataset. In our experiments, we have used two datasets (see Fig. 4). The first dataset contains 155 multispectral images (NIR, Red) plus the NDVI index acquired in a *sugar beets* field. It is provided with pixel-wise annotations into three classes (crop, weed, and soil). The second dataset contains 75 multispectral images acquired in a *corn* field, with pixel-wise annotations into two classes (soil, and plant). We used 100 images of the first dataset for training after a data augmentation process. In particular, we applied rotations, horizontal and vertical flipping to create an augmented training dataset composed by 420 images. The remaining 55 images from the original dataset were used for testing purposes. The second dataset containing *corn* images was used for testing only. We evaluated the generalization capability of the net for classifying the pixels in two classes, namely soil and plant.

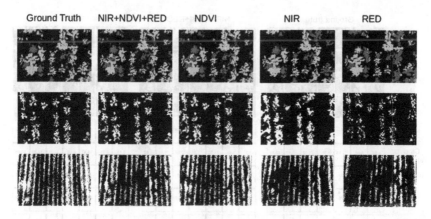

Fig. 5. Qualitative results achieved by CNN with different input type. First and second rows represent the output for 3 classes segmentation on sugar beet dataset, the third row 2 classes segmentation output on corn dataset.

Table 1. Quantitative results illustrating mean accuracy obtained by VGG-UNet using different input on the sugar beets and corn datasets.

Input	3-classes	2-classes	
	Sugar beet	Sugar beet	Corn
Red	0.84	0.91	0.73
NIR	0.90	0.96	0.85
NDVI	0.93	**0.99**	**0.92**
RED+NIR+NDVI	**0.95**	0.98	0.88

Table 2. Quantitative results illustrating mean accuracy obtained by SegNet and VGG-UNet architectures on the sugar beet dataset.

Architecture	3-classes RED+NIR+NDVI input	2-classes NDVI input
SegNet	0.93	0.98
VGG-UNet	**0.95**	**0.99**

Network Training. We trained the proposed VGG-UNet by initializing the encoder (VGG-16) with the weights taken from training the VGG-16 on the ImageNet dataset, then we trained the whole network using Stochastic Gradient Descent (SGD) with a fixed learning rate of $1 \cdot e^{-4}$ and a momentum of 0.90. The parameters of the network are updated in a way that cross entropy loss is reduced. Mini-batches composed by one image was used for training.

Evaluation. Qualitative results of using different input types for pixel-wise segmentation into soil, weed, and crop on sugar beet dataset are shown in the first

Ground truth   **NIR+NDVI+RED**   **NDVI**

Crop Distribution

Ground truth:

13.59	14.24	5.0	4.9	22.72	15.79	15.18
5.22	3.96	11.89	8.36	24.02	10.47	12.28
11.24	34.28	5.77	4.73	2.35	10.11	14.62
10.85	25.98	5.26	8.39	10.54	15.12	33.52

NIR+NDVI+RED:

10.14	14.24	2.02	2.34	33.24	24.87	8.4
0.0	3.68	14.06	11.24	30.07	18.84	1.88
10.82	35.56	13.38	12.34	1.53	20.1	8.57
6.39	22.97	1.27	10.8	10.25	21.86	35.47

NDVI:

16.81	17.46	4.69	6.5	36.37	24.96	19.97
5.41	3.81	18.47	8.95	31.95	17.37	10.48
14.6	41.74	10.38	10.96	4.46	19.17	20.73
13.33	32.71	8.08	15.8	14.75	25.99	46.09

weed Distribution

Ground truth:

9.65	4.69	4.69	4.72	4.69	4.74	13.65
5.21	12.58	0.1	0.07	0.8	0.26	9.39
7.74	0.81	3.0	0.02	2.16	0.0	10.06
9.65	4.71	11.06	8.43	4.77	6.15	15.98

NIR+NDVI+RED:

4.09	6.07	2.91	2.52	1.56	2.58	1.75
0.0	22.96	2.7	1.84	4.85	2.76	3.38
8.86	6.37	2.38	0.46	11.9	0.23	1.55
0.27	1.58	14.18	5.79	1.31	2.18	4.29

NDVI:

12.78	5.05	5.02	5.08	4.72	6.67	13.92
5.24	21.92	0.5	5.18	5.63	2.9	13.94
13.27	7.54	5.38	1.49	8.33	0.0	11.4
12.05	7.14	18.26	14.15	12.04	10.7	19.98

Fig. 6. Results from computing weed and crop distribution with different input types. The first column represent the ground truth. The second and third columns shows the prediction output from VGG-UNet when using NIR+NDVI+RED and NDVI as input. The second and third rows represents crop and weed distribution. (Color figure online)

row of Fig. 5. The segmentation performance of VGG-UNet decreased when we used Red channel alone as input. The best results was achieved using the three channels together as input, while for pixel-wise segmentation into soil, and plant sugar beet dataset the best result for NDVI channel. Table 1 shows the quantitative results obtained by the used VGG-UNet architecture. We have performed also a quantitative comparison between the used VGG-UNet architecture and the SegNet network. Table 2 contains the results for the comparison. VGG-UNet performs slightly better on the sugar beet dataset.

The final output of our approach is shown in Fig. 6, where the first row shows the segmentation output, the second and third rows show the crop and weed distribution. The number in each cell describes the crop distribution (in the second row) and the weed distribution (in the third row). The green circles show the high density of crop, while the red ones show the high density of weed. The performance of VGG-UNet architecture has been tested on an embedded GPU board, namely Jetson TX2, and the processing time per image was 0.6 s when we use three channels together as input, and around 0.2 s when we used each channel alone as input.

5   Conclusion

In this paper, we addressed the problem of crop/weeds distribution estimation in UAV multi-spectral imagery. We tackled the problem by proposing a two-step approach that leverages a Convolutional Neural Network to perform image semantic segmentation and a post-processing step to compute the crop/weed statistics. We reported experiments on two datasets with different crop types, and by using different multi-spectral inputs. The results confirm the effectiveness of the proposed solutions.

References

1. Badrinarayanan, V., Kendall, A., Cipolla, R.: SegNet: a deep convolutional encoder-decoder architecture for image segmentation. IEEE Trans. Pattern Anal. Mach. Intell. **39**(12), 2481–2495 (2017)
2. Burks, T.F., Shearer, S.A., Gates, R.S., Donohue, K.D.: Backpropagation neural network design and evaluation for classifying weed species using color image texture. Trans. ASAE **43**(4), 1029–1037 (2000)
3. Di Cicco, M., Potena, C., Grisetti, G., Pretto, A.: Automatic model based dataset generation for fast and accurate crop and weeds detection. In: IROS, pp. 5188–5195 (2017)
4. Fawakherji, M., Youssef, A., Bloisi, D.D., Pretto, A., Nardi, D.: Crop and weeds classification for precision agriculture using context-independent pixel-wise segmentation. In: 2019 Third IEEE International Conference on Robotic Computing (IRC), pp. 146–152 (2019). https://doi.org/10.1109/IRC.2019.00029
5. Haug, S., Michaels, A., Biber, P., Ostermann, J.: Plant classification system for crop/weed discrimination without segmentation. In: Proceedings of the IEEE Winter Conference on Applications of Computer Vision (WACV) (2014)
6. Hemming, J., Rath, T.: PA-precision agriculture: computer-vision-based weed identification under field conditions using controlled lighting. J. Agric. Eng. Res. **78**(3), 233–243 (2001)
7. Lottes, P., Behley, J., Milioto, A., Stachniss, C.: Fully convolutional networks with sequential information for robust crop and weed detection in precision farming. IEEE Robot. Autom. Lett. **3**(4), 2870–2877 (2018)
8. Lottes, P., Hoeferlin, M., Sander, S., Müter, M., Schulze, P., Stachniss, L.C.: An effective classification system for separating sugar beets and weeds for precision farming applications. In: 2016 IEEE International Conference on Robotics and Automation (ICRA), pp. 5157–5163, May 2016
9. Lottes, P., Khanna, R., Pfeifer, J., Siegwart, R., Stachniss, C.: UAV-based crop and weed classification for smart farming. In: 2017 IEEE International Conference on Robotics and Automation (ICRA), pp. 3024–3031, May 2017
10. Milioto, A., Lottes, P., Stachniss, C.: Real-time semantic segmentation of crop and weed for precision agriculture robots leveraging background knowledge in CNNs. In: 2018 IEEE International Conference on Robotics and Automation (ICRA), pp. 2229–2235, May 2018
11. Potena, C., Nardi, D., Pretto, A.: Fast and accurate crop and weed identification with summarized train sets for precision agriculture. In: Chen, W., Hosoda, K., Menegatti, E., Shimizu, M., Wang, H. (eds.) IAS 2016. AISC, vol. 531, pp. 105–121. Springer, Cham (2017). https://doi.org/10.1007/978-3-319-48036-7_9

12. Ronneberger, O., Fischer, P., Brox, T.: U-net: convolutional networks for biomedical image segmentation. arXiv abs/1505.04597 (2015)
13. Sa, I., et al.: weedNet: dense semantic weed classification using multispectral images and mav for smart farming. IEEE Robot. Autom. Lett. 3(1), 588–595 (2018)
14. Sa, I., et al.: WeedMap: a large-scale semantic weed mapping framework using aerial multispectral imaging and deep neural network for precision farming. Remote Sens. 10, 1423 (2018)
15. Shearer, S.A., Holmes, R.G.: Plant identification using color co-occurrence matrices. Trans. ASAE 33(6), 2037–2044 (1990)

An Integrated Precision Farming Application Based on 5G, UAV and Deep Learning Technologies

Manzoor Razaak[1]([✉]), Hamideh Kerdegari[1], Eleanor Davies[2],
Raouf Abozariba[2], Matthew Broadbent[2], Katy Mason[2], Vasileios Argyriou[1],
and Paolo Remagnino[1]

[1] The Robot Vision Team, Kingston University, London, UK
{manzoor.razaak,h.kerdegari,vasileios.argyriou,
p.remagnino}@kingston.ac.uk
[2] Lancaster University, Lancaster, UK
{eleanor.davies,r.abozariba,m.broadbent,k.j.mason}@lancaster.co.uk

Abstract. Wireless communication technology has made tremendous progress over the last two decades providing extensive coverage, high data-rate and low-latency. The current major upgrade, the fifth generation (5G) wireless technology promises substantial improvement over 4G broadband cellular technology. However, even in many developed countries, rural areas are significantly under-connected with mobile wireless technology. Developing 5G testbeds in rural areas can provide an incentive for service providers to improve internet connectivity. 5G Rural Integrated Testbed (5GRIT) is a project commissioned to develop testbeds for 5G in rural areas in the United Kingdom (UK). The project aims to demonstrate the role 5G networks can play in empowering farming and tourism sectors using an integrated system of unmanned aerial vehicles (UAV) and artificial intelligence technologies. This paper reports some of the studies and findings of the 5GRIT project, specifically, the results of testbed implementation and the deep learning algorithms developed for precision farming applications.

Keywords: Unmanned aerial vehicles (UAV) · Deep learning · 5G · Precision farming · 5GRIT

1 Introduction

5G Rural Integrated Testbed (5GRIT) is a partnership of small and medium-sized enterprises and Universities for building a 5G testbeds to develop and test solutions for rural areas [1]. The project's vision encompasses compelling

---

The research leading to these results have received funding from the Department for Digital, Culture, Media & Sports (DCMS), United Kingdom, under its 5G trials and testbeds program.

© Springer Nature Switzerland AG 2019
M. Vento and G. Percannella (Eds.): CAIP 2019 Workshops, CCIS 1089, pp. 109–119, 2019.
https://doi.org/10.1007/978-3-030-29930-9_11

use cases for 5G technologies, applications and services delivering benefits in rural areas. The project construct several 5G testbeds in rural areas in the UK including Cumbria, Northumberland, North Yorkshire. The TV White Space (TVWS) technology is used to test the potential of shared spectrum radio to deliver 5G services to rural areas and test the capabilities of 5G. An important objective for the project is to develop agricultural applications on an integrated technological platform of UAV, image sensors, 5G data transfer and artificial intelligence.

Figure 1 illustrates the precision farming system envisioned under 5GRIT. The integrated system enables UAV to capture aerial images of the crop and livestock for transmission using 5G to a video analytics server. The deep learning based algorithms analyze the imagery for potential applications such as crop health monitoring, crop-weed classification, livestock detection and location, activity monitoring and anomaly detection.

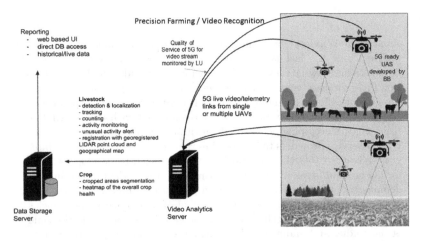

Fig. 1. A precision farming system envisioned under the 5GRIT project.

This paper describes the objectives and the findings of the 5GRIT project. Section 2 outlines the implementation of 5G testbeds in rural areas. Section 3 describes the precision farming applications developed and studied in the project. Both sections outlines the implementation and its findings. Section 4 concludes the paper.

2   5G Testbed Implementation and Evaluation

In many parts of the globe, including developed countries, there remains large pockets where internet is unavailable or available with limited service quality, making many applications and services inaccessible. This is largely the result of failure of previous generation of cellular networks such as 3G and 4G to reach to rural areas combined with lack of incentives from major internet service providers to roll-out wired broadband coverage such as xDSL and fibre.

As a consequence, various solutions are emerging, including those which are powered by TVWS and mmWave spectrum as alternative means for rural broadband expansion. These solutions are considered to be economical and provide adequate quality of service (QoS), however, detailed information on these solutions are limited and it is essential to analyze the effectiveness of such solutions in providing diverse services to a broad range of applications.

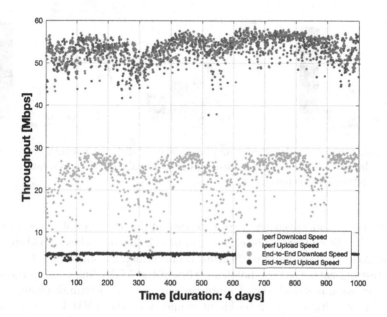

Fig. 2. TVWS speed tests.

The 5GRIT project explores the TVWS and mmWave spectrum for 5G by monitoring and evaluating the technology in rural areas of the United Kingdom. Specific testbeds in rural areas across UK were identified to implement both TVWS and mmWave spectrum technologies. The deployment of equipment came in two phases: the first phase included installation of TVWS equipment in three rural locations. Since non-line-of-sight is one of the key aspects of TVWS, locations were chosen to test the viability of transverse hills and trees.

The TVWS successfully delivers dual channel double digit speed connections, and therefore is able to support interactive applications developed under the project [6]. On the other hand, the mmWave solution was installed into a housing estate, which was serviced with below 2 Mbps internet services and no sign of emerging fibre installation. The installation enabled to deliver high speed connectivity.

The performance of the TVWS and the mmWave equipment was monitored and evaluated using different performance metrics. The throughput capacity on

a network operating on TVWS channels was evaluated using a passive monitoring. Figure 2 presents the throughput of 1000 measuring instances performed
over four days. The upload/download speed of the wireless TVWS link between
the user and the TVWS base station is shown. Measurements covering the entire
connection, which consists of 10 km 5 GHz backhaul link were also taken. From
the figure it is evident that the TVWS technology operating over two 8 MHz
bonded channels can support up to 58 Mbps upload/download speed on a symmetric link.

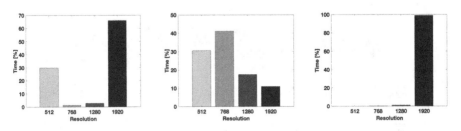

Fig. 3. Comparison of video streaming performance of different networks. (left) ADSL
video resolution. (middle) TVWS with 5 GHz backhaul link video resolution. (right)
mmWave network video resolution.

The end-to-end speed tests provide insight on the overall effective speed
perceived by the end user. The end-to-end uplink speed reaches 5.93 Mbps while
the download speed is close to 29 Mbps on asymmetric connection. The output
of this test indicates that the bottleneck lies in the 5 GHz link causing the speed
to be split asymmetrical giving more capacity to the downlink channel. This
suggests that with a better backhaul connection, the TVWS is a promising
solution which potentially substitutes traditional wired broadband solutions. A
noteworthy observation is that no outages occurred demonstrating the good
stability of the service. The passive monitoring of the network showed that the
signal strength fluctuation patterns are stable within a desired range (between
−72 and −75 dB). Further, the TVWS deployment also demonstrated very low
latency and jitter throughout the monitoring period.

The mmWave radios are known to provide high capacity and high-speed
data transmission and in our studies it achieved speed that was 4–5 times faster
than its TVWS counterpart. The quality of experience (QoE) of both TVWS
and mmWave for adaptive video streaming was evaluated. 48 identical videos
files were transmitted over the internet over two days. Due to the super-fast
internet speed provided by the mmWave technology, the resolution is almost
perfect with 98.9% of the frames are transmitted using the 1920p resolution—the
highest available option—with just over 1% of the total time is spent between the
720p and 1280p resolutions. The TVWS transmitted the highest resolution for
approximately 11% of the transmission, 41.1% of the total time, the videos were
transmitted using the 768p resolution and 70% of the total time in the higher

three resolutions. The adaptive video streaming performance was compared with the standard ADSL network, as shown in Fig. 3.

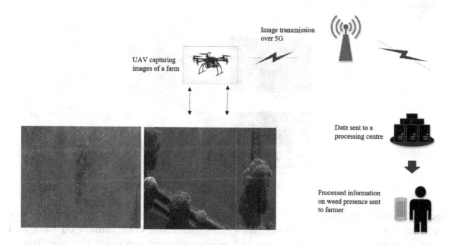

UAV capturing
images of a farm

Image transmission
over 5G

Data sent to a
processing centre

Processed information
on weed presence sent
to farmer

Fig. 4. A weed/livestock detection system comprising of a UAV with a mounted multispectral/RGB camera, 5G transmission system, and a data processing centre hosting the captured image data and weed detection algorithms.

3   Precision Farming Based on UAV and Deep Learning

An important goal for 5GRIT project was to demonstrate the capabilities of 5G for smart farming applications. The project envisaged a data acquisition and transmission system mounted on a UAV to capture aerial imagery of the farms and transmit the farm images over 5G for artificial intelligence based computer vision analysis.

An illustration of the aerial crop/livestock monitoring system used in our project is presented in Fig. 4. The system includes a UAV to capture images of the farm to provide as an input data for the deep learning based computer vision algorithms that are designed to detect presence of weed/livestock. The algorithms process the images at a data processing center and transmit the outcomes to the concerned stakeholders, such as a farmer.

Based on the literature, discussions with stakeholders and feasibility analysis, algorithms were designed for two use cases. The use cases were split into two main areas, crop management and livestock monitoring, and specifically two applications were designed and developed: crop-weed classification and livestock detection.

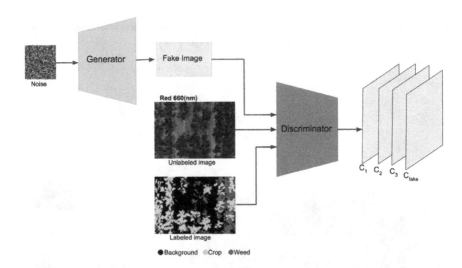

Fig. 5. The semi-supervised GAN architecture. Random noise is used by the Generator to generate an image. The Discriminator uses generated data, unlabeled data and labeled data to learn class confidences and produces confidence maps for each class as well as a label for a fake data.

3.1 Crop-Weed Classification

For the crop monitoring use case, the focus was on management of in-field variability in order to enable farmers to move from a prophylactic approach to crop protection and move to a more targeted approach to weed control with the help of UAV. To do so required the capturing of the crop images from a UAV at multiple times during a full cropping season with two imaging sensors, multispectral and RGB sensors.

Deep learning algorithms were developed for crop-weed classification from the multispectral images of the farm captured by UAV. The developed approach is based on the generative adversarial networks (GAN) [3]. Deep learning methods require very large corpus of data for training and hence to generate sufficient amount of data for algorithm training, GAN algorithm is employed. Particularly, the semi-supervised GAN method that is explored to generate additional multispectral corpus for training the crop-weed classification algorithm.

A traditional GAN has a generator and discriminator. In the semi-supervised GAN, the discriminator is replaced with a multiclass classifier, which, instead of predicting whether a sample x belongs to the data distribution (real or fake), it assigns to each input image pixel a label y from the n classes (i.e. crop, weed or background) or mark it as a fake sample (extra $n+1$ class).

Figure 5 presents a schematic description of the semi-supervised GAN architecture that three inputs such as generated multispectral data, unlabeled data and a small number of labeled data are fed into the discriminator.

Results. The proposed semi-supervised GAN algorithm is evaluated on the weedNet [8] dataset collected by a micro aerial vehicle (MAV) equipped with a 4-band Sequoia multispectral camera. The multispectral images are captured from sugar beets field at 2 m height. The dataset contains only NIR and Red channel due to difficulties in image registration of other bands. From corresponding NIR and Red channel images, the Normalized NDVI is extracted to indicate the difference between soil and plant. Therefore, each training/test image consists of the 790 nm NIR channel, the 660 nm red channel, and NDVI imagery. The dataset contains only crops, or weeds, or crop-weed combination along with their corresponding pixel-wise annotated data.

| Red | NIR | NDVI | Semi-supervised | Annotated Image |

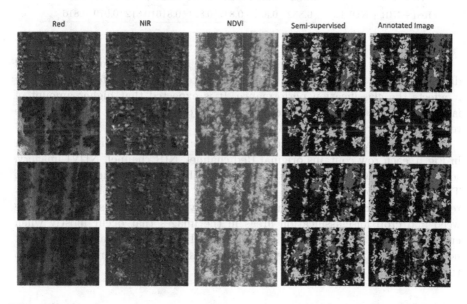

Fig. 6. Qualitative results for the weedNet test set. The first three columns are input data to the semi-supervised GAN, the fourth is the results of semi-supervised GAN using 30% of labeled data and the last column is ground truth. (Color figure online)

For semi-supervised training, different percentages of pixel-wise annotated images (such as 50%, 40% and 30%) are used as labeled data to the discriminator and the rest of images are without pixel-wise annotations. The performance accuracy of crop-weed classification is calculated through the standard F1 score. Quantitative results of our method on weedNet are shown in Table 1.

Considering the challenges in the dataset, all models (including different channels + different amount of labeled data) perform reasonably well (about 80% for all classes). As shown in Table 1, two input channels (Red and NIR) yield higher performance compared to single channels as they contain more useful features to be used by the semi-supervised GAN network. However, using 3 channels (NDVI + Red + NIR) did not improve performance as NDVI depends on NIR and red channels rather than capturing new information.

Table 1. Results on the weedNet dataset using 50%, 40% and 30% of labeled data with different number of channels for semi-supervised GAN, and cascaded CNN [8] with fully labeled data. Higher F1 values indicate better classification performance.

F1 score	Semi-supervised GAN						Cascaded CNN	
Amount of labeled data	50%		40%		30%		Fully labeled	
Channel	Crop	Weed	Crop	Weed	Crop	Weed	Crop	Weed
Red	0.831	0.814	0.822	0.813	0.792	0.813	0.923	0.845
NIR	0.839	0.823	0.80	0.821	0.782	0.733	0.942	0.839
NDVI	0.826	0.803	0.817	0.79	0.788	0.812	0.952	0.849
Red + NIR	**0.857**	**0.865**	0.837	0.834	0.823	0.815	0.971	0.851
Red + NIR + NDVI	0.852	0.831	0.847	0.821	0.816	0.812	0.979	0.816

Furthermore, the network was evaluated by reducing the amount of labeled data starting at 50% and then reducing by step 10 to 30% to find out how it affects the classification performance. It is expected that higher amount of labeled data result in better performance. It can be seen by comparing the results of the 50%, 40% and 30% in Table 1.

The qualitative evaluation is performed on four sample test images. As shown in Fig. 6, each row contains original Red channel, NIR channel, NDVI imagery, semi-supervised GAN probability output and the corresponding ground truth. The probability of each class is mapped to the red, green and black color representing weed, crop and background, respectively. There are some noticeable weed and crop misclassification areas in the images that occur mostly when crops and weeds are surrounded by each other. This misclassification shows that network can capture high-level features such as shape and texture in addition to the low-level features.

3.2   Livestock Monitoring

The use case aims at developing algorithms capable of livestock detection and counting from aerial images captured by drones. State-of-the-art object detection algorithms were adapted and implemented for the livestock detection algorithm. Aerial images of livestock from a drone flown at 50 m altitude were captured at a farm.

At higher altitudes, the mounted cameras capture lower resolution images and the target such as livestock are represented in small sizes in the images that pose challenges for computer vision analysis. Generally, small size targets in images have lower feature representations and provides limited learning information for machine learning algorithms. Our studies showed that recent deep learning methods based on convolutional neural networks (CNN) such as Fast-CNN [2] and you only look once (YOLO) [7] that have demonstrated high detection accuracy, however, usually perform better with large targets than small targets in the images. Both YOLO and Fast-CNN performed poorly with livestock detection in our UAV images.

The multiscale feature based object detectors have shown better performance in small object detection. The single shot multibox detection (SSD) is one of the popular multi-scale based object detector. To improve the livestock detection accuracy, we explored the Single Shot Multibox Detector (SSD) algorithm [5]. SSD is a popular, state-of-the-art object detection algorithm that achieves very fast and better object detection accuracy than several other popular algorithms. Figure 7 represents the network architecture of the SSD algorithm.

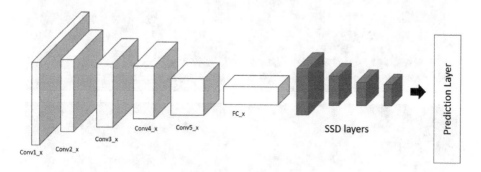

Fig. 7. Network architecture of SSD object detector.

A common method in deep learning algorithms is to use "deeper layers" that represent an object with abstract features for prediction. Thus, in such systems, small objects are not sufficiently represented by the feature maps and hence the predictors such as YOLO that mainly consider the features at the deeper layers fail to make accurate predictions [4]. An inherent feature of the SSD algorithm is that it uses feature maps from different scales in the network for predicting objects. This feature along with other improvements in the algorithm, allows the SSD detector to perform better on small object detection. In our study, we applied the SSD algorithm to evaluate its performance in object detection and achieved a higher detection accuracy of around 72%. The details of our study are provided below.

Experiment Results. A UAV captured 425 images of livestock at a farm with a very high image resolution of 5472 × 3648 pixels. For object detection, ground truth data consists of pixel coordinates of bounding box around the objects of interest. The ground truth was generated through crowdsourcing via the Amazon Mechanical Turks platform.

Deep learning algorithms require high computational processing resources for training and learning the ability to detect objects. Very high resolution images cannot be used as computers cannot handle such high data. Therefore, the original livestock images were split into 300 × 300 pixel resolution and we obtained approximately 3000 images that consisted of livestock.

For training, 80% of the dataset was used as a training dataset and 20% was used for validation. The SSD algorithm was trained on an Nvidia Graphical

Fig. 8. Collage of detection results using SSD algorithm.

Processing Unit (GPU). The results of our study showed that an accuracy of around 72% was achieved with SSD algorithm which is a significant improvement of 57% accuracy from the YOLO object detection method. Samples of output are shown in Fig. 8.

In Fig. 8, it can be noted that our trained SSD algorithm performs well at detecting livestock. However, it misses detecting some of the sheep in the images. A detailed evaluation of the SSD implementation showed that SSD was able to detect livestock with an accuracy of around 72%, hence some of the missed detections. The detection performance of SSD can be further improved. Various techniques are being explored to improve the accuracy of detection. This includes improving the volume of the training dataset and custom tailoring the SSD model to work with higher accuracy for our objective.

4   Conclusion

The 5GRIT project enabled to get greater understanding of advent 5G broadband technologies. The project does not only offer new insights into 5G deployments and performance characterization but it paves the way to provide sustainable and affordable connectivity to thousands of homes and businesses across the rural areas of the UK. A full-stack monitoring framework capable of providing analysis and performance evaluation of 5G fixed wireless broadband technologies was developed and tested. The project demonstrated the potential of using 5G enabled drones equipped with cameras to monitor farm lands to reduce human intervention in the farms. The deep learning based UAV image analysis algorithms show that precision farming can greatly benefit from an integrated system of UAV, artificial intelligence and 5G technologies. The planned future work includes conducting more UAV flights to acquire crop images at different stages of its growth cycle for developing more precision farming applications.

References

1. 5G Rural Integrated Testbed. http://www.5grit.co.uk/. Accessed 01 July 2019
2. Girshick, R.: Fast R-CNN. In: Proceedings of the IEEE International Conference on Computer Vision, pp. 1440–1448 (2015)
3. Goodfellow, I., et al.: Generative adversarial nets. In: Advances in Neural Information Processing Systems, pp. 2672–2680 (2014)
4. Lin, T.Y., Dollár, P., Girshick, R., He, K., Hariharan, B., Belongie, S.: Feature pyramid networks for object detection. In: Proceedings of the IEEE Conference on Computer Vision and Pattern Recognition, pp. 2117–2125 (2017)
5. Liu, W., et al.: SSD: single shot MultiBox detector. In: Leibe, B., Matas, J., Sebe, N., Welling, M. (eds.) ECCV 2016. LNCS, vol. 9905, pp. 21–37. Springer, Cham (2016). https://doi.org/10.1007/978-3-319-46448-0_2
6. Mitola, J.: Accelerating 5G QoE via public-private spectrum sharing. IEEE Commun. Mag. **52**(5), 77–85 (2014)
7. Redmon, J., Divvala, S., Girshick, R., Farhadi, A.: You only look once: unified, real-time object detection. In: Proceedings of the IEEE Conference on Computer Vision and Pattern Recognition, pp. 779–788 (2016)
8. Sa, I., et al.: weedNet: dense semantic weed classification using multispectral images and MAV for smart farming. IEEE Robot. Autom. Lett. **3**(1), 588–595 (2017)

Visual Communication with UAV: Use Cases and Achievements

Alexander Schelle and Peter Stütz[✉]

University of the Bundeswehr Munich, 85577 Neubiberg, Germany
{alexander.schelle, peter.stuetz}@unibw.de

Abstract. This paper illustrates an alternative approach towards mission control of UAV beyond the usage of radio data link. It is based on bidirectional visual communication employing onboard computer vision to recognize the operator's gestures and providing visible feedback to him. This work presents use cases and summarizes the achievements made so far at the Institute of Flight Systems with respect to functional concepts, system architectures, sensor technology, data processing and experimental validation.

Keywords: Visual communication · Gesture recognition · Human-UAV-interaction

1 Motivation

Today's unmanned aerial vehicles are primarily used as sensor platforms for area surveillance, in the search missions for persons and vehicles and for cartographic purposes [1]. However, to function properly, they require a wireless data link to a ground control station or a mobile device. By using an active radio-based form of communication, there is always the danger of connection disturbances and breakdowns due to topographical conditions or targeted influence by third parties. The emission of an electromagnetic signature can also be undesirable or dangerous in certain applications.

Therefore, we made it our task to design and investigate alternatives. We envision a communication system that is fundamentally independent of ground-based infrastructure and is based on machine interpretation of body language together with visual feedback from the UAV. While the recognition of individual gestures on board the UAV is already used to trigger simple reactions [2–4], it is our goal to transfer complex mission tasks.

2 Use Cases and System Architectures

A number of use cases for the application of visual communication between UAV platforms and people on the ground have been established. These include the following:

1. Persons belonging to the guidance loop of the UAV:
   (a) Control of take-off and landing commands: In this case, operators command and control the take-off, but above all the landing process of UAV. The interaction

© Springer Nature Switzerland AG 2019
M. Vento and G. Percannella (Eds.): CAIP 2019 Workshops, CCIS 1089, pp. 120–128, 2019.
https://doi.org/10.1007/978-3-030-29930-9_12

with the operators serves for the direct control of the movement of the platform, the assignment of a touchdown point or the imitation as well as the abort of the landing process.

(b) Transmission of mission orders: Here, people transmit complex mission orders by means of gestures and visual feedback. Such missions can include transport, reconnaissance or manipulation tasks, which must be parameterized and consist of a sequence of mission phases.

2. Persons not belonging to the guidance loop of the UAV:

(a) Identification and interviewing of persons: In this application, a UAV establishes bidirectional communication with detected persons. The aim is, for example, to determine their identity and state of health.

(b) Evacuation of persons: In this application, a UAV establishes a bidirectional communication with detected persons on the ground. The aim is, for example, to lead people out of a dangerous area along a safe path.

Figure 1 gives a schematic impression of a surveillance mission performed by a UAV system tasked via gestures.

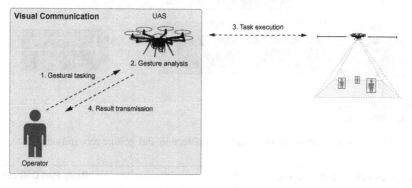

Fig. 1. Illustration of use case 1b [5]

Figure 2 visualizes the basic system components involved.

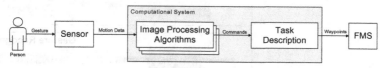

Fig. 2. Basic functional components for issuing navigational commands based on gestures [5]

In [5] a first system concept was presented introducing two general operating modes (see Fig. 3). In detection mode potential communication counterparts are identified, tracked and, if needed, checked for authentication. After successful detection, the system changes to interaction mode, where gestures and pose are recognized and translated into command components. The architecture at the time considered the usage of 3D-depth sensors, which changed later.

In [6] a second-generation architecture now relying on both depth and infrared data and introducing a dedicated functional block for body part detection separate from gesture recognition (Fig. 4).

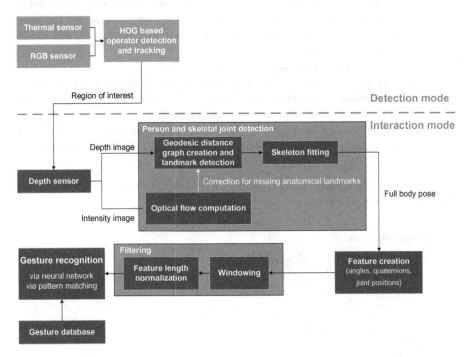

Fig. 3. First system architecture for counterpart detection and gesture recognition approach [5]

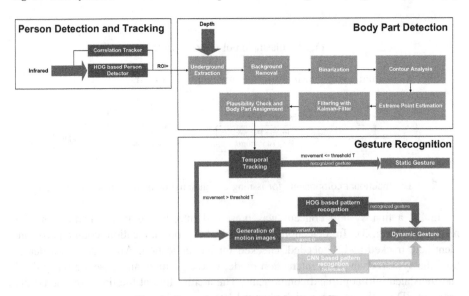

Fig. 4. Second-generation architecture [6]

3 Sensors and Gesture Recognition

In a first implementation [6] Intel RealSense R200 camera was selected for data acquisition. It featured a multisensory all-in-one solution with a high-resolution color sensor but also two infrared sensitive sensors in a stereoscopic setup to generate 3-D depth data (Fig. 5).

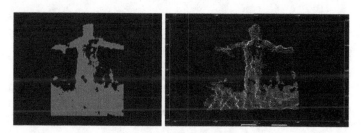

Fig. 5. 2D-matrix (left) and 3D-point cloud (right) depiction from single and stereo IR-sensor [6]

Expectations were high to exploit the computationally more demanding 3D-point cloud data for more detailed gesture and pose recognition, however outdoor experiments revealed the sensors maximum depth range of about 10 m with a rapidly decreasing depth accuracy on that end of the operational area.

Meanwhile [7] commonly available 2D image sensors avoiding the limitations of depth sensors are used allowing a feasible communication distance of up to 50 m utilizing a 1080p sensor with a 20x optical zoom lens. However, the limiting factor here is the recognizability of the visual feedback device by the human operator. In experiments, distances of about 25 m have proven to be a good compromise between readability for a 32 × 8 cm LED matrix and a safe distance to the flying system.

The image data of the camera is processed with the OpenPose framework [8], which utilizes a Convolutional Neural Network for body part detection and so called Part Affinity Fields for part association to assemble a full body pose (Fig. 6 left). To boost the processing speed, hardware supporting CUDA [9] is used onboard the UAV. To allow the transmission of numerical information, a hand-finger detection based on the analysis of convexity defects of the detected hand contours (Fig. 6 right) was implemented [10].

Fig. 6. Joint information provided by OpenPose (left) and visualization of the onboard gesture recognition and finger detection (right) from [7]

4   Feedback Mechanisms

Figure 7 from [5] presents a first idea on a visual feedback mechanism at small distances based on LED lights for the interaction mode. The latest version feedback mechanism to enable bidirectional communication was presented in [7] using a 32 × 8 LED matrix (Fig. 8).

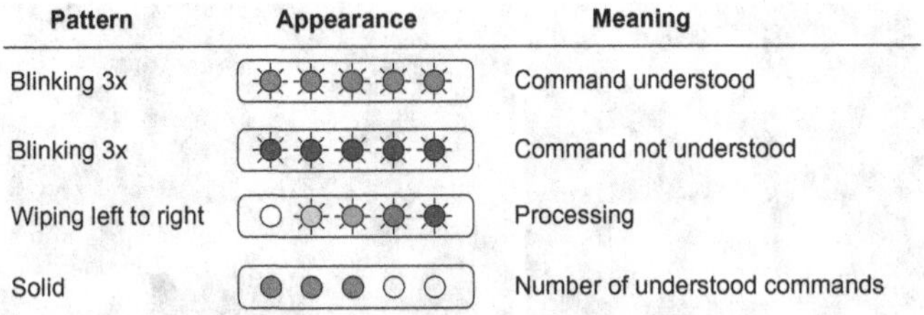

Pattern	Appearance	Meaning
Blinking 3x		Command understood
Blinking 3x		Command not understood
Wiping left to right		Processing
Solid		Number of understood commands

Fig. 7. First visual feedback system [5]

Fig. 8. Multicopter UAV with stabilized sensor system, processing board and LED matrix for visual feedback [7]

5   Gesture Models and Experimental Validations

With the system described in [7] the following tasking commands (Fig. 9) can be derived from detected and processed static gestures using a feature comparison approach. To allow the processing of dynamic gestures foreseen as well, preliminary test were made showing that the currently achieved frame rate of 4.5 fps is not sufficient. A hardware upgrade shall yield the necessary performance boost in future.

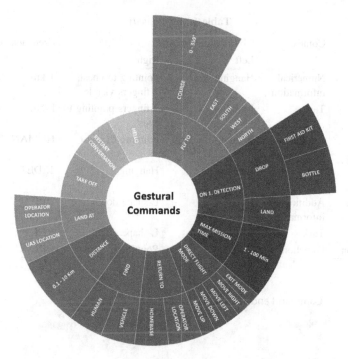

Fig. 9. Supported gestural tasking commands and the task dependent additional information from [7]

In [7] the basic system capability was tested following a guided conversation protocol using mutual gesture recognition and visual feedback. Table 1 shows an exemplary mission to be commanded by a test person. Figures 10 and 11 show sequenced question – answer pairs.

Table 1. Exemplary mission

Meaning	Context	Observation for Arm		Feedback	Question
		Left	Right		
Conversation start	None	Hanging	L-shape up	HELLO	TASK?
Fly	Task	Pointing out	Pointing out	FLY	TO?
Course	Direction	Palm touching other palm, low	Palm touching other palm, low	CRS	C —
1	Numerical information	Hanging	Pointing to chest, 1 finger visible	C 1-	
2	Numerical information	Hanging	Pointing to chest, 2 fingers visible	C 12-	
2	Numerical information	Hanging	Pointing to chest, 2 fingers visible	C 122	DIST?

(continued)

Table 1. (*continued*)

Meaning	Context	Observation for Arm		Feedback	Question
		Left	Right		
For 1 km	Numerical information	Hanging	Pointing to chest, 2 fingers visible	1 km	THEN?
Find	Task	Hanging	2 fingers pointing to eyes	FIND	WHAT?
Human	Additional information	Pointing to chest	Pointing to chest	HUMAN	THEN?
On first detection	Task	L-shape up	Hanging	1. DET	DO?
Drop bottle	Additional information	Hanging	L-shape down	DRP B	THEN?
Return to	Task	L-shape down	L-shape down	RET	LOC?
My location	Direction	Hanging	Pointing to ground	URLOC	OK

Fig. 10. Operator tasking UAV to fly to a specific direction, UAV responds with question

Fig. 11. Operator tasks UAV to perform an action on the first detection of a human, UAV asks for the action

Figure 12 shows the specific response times for various non-numerical and numerical single gestural commands. All time measurements start in neutral pose, i.e. both arms are hanging, and stop once the LED matrix displays a feedback. So, this measurement includes the transformation from the neutral pose to the final gesture. The experiments were conducted with the recognition system mounted on an airborne multicopter. Results concerning the system fixed in a lab environment showed noticeable better results.

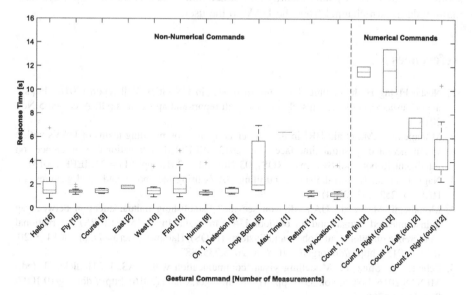

Fig. 12. Response times for gestural commands from first movement to display for airborne setup, delay of pose estimation not included [7]

In a recent experiment, a new method for a systematic encoding of verbal commands into gestural utterances for commanding UAVs was evaluated [11]. In this approach, graphical symbols were used as motion templates for dynamic gestures. It was examined whether the use of a symbolically motivated gesture vocabulary has positive effects on the memory performance and reproducibility of the operator's gestures. The new approach provided higher reproductive accuracy, but it took the subjects a little longer to remember the gestures.

6 Conclusion

In the future, unmanned aerial vehicles will mostly be operated remotely or move autonomously. They will inevitably have to interact with their environment and the people inside it. With the help of visual communication, it is now possible for third parties that were previously outside the control loop to interact with the flying system (e.g. isolated units that require reconnaissance data but do not have the appropriate command or control devices). The resulting transfer of authority via the flying system to any person opens up completely new possibilities. For instance, the unmanned system can be made available for a limited period of time and/or locally as an airborne resource for an authorized person or group. An important element for a natural interaction is the development of a suitable conversation structure, which on the one hand allows a free formulation of the mission task, but on the other hand also considers the available computing power and the capabilities of the UAV. Likewise, new methods should be explored to visually identify authorized individuals as well as new ways for a multimodal return channel from the UAV to the user.

References

1. Nesta: Flying High: shaping the future of drones in UK cities. Full report (2018). https://media.nesta.org.uk/documents/Flying-High-full-report-and-appendices.pdf. Accessed 5 Nov 2018
2. Monajjemi, V.M., et al.: HRI in the sky: creating and commanding teams of UAVs with a vision-mediated gestural interface. In: 2013 IEEE/RSJ International Conference on Intelligent Robots and Systems (IROS), 03 November 2013, pp. 617–623. IEEE (2013)
3. Nagi, J., et al.: HRI in the sky: controlling UAVs using face poses and hand gestures. In: HRI, pp. 252–253 (2014)
4. Monajjemi, M., et al.: UAV, do you see me? Establishing mutual attention between an uninstrumented human and an outdoor UAV in flight. In: 2015 IEEE/RSJ International Conference on Intelligent Robots and Systems (IROS), Hamburg, Germany, pp. 3614–3620. IEEE (2015). https://doi.org/10.1109/iros.2015.7353882
5. Schelle, A., Stütz, P.: Modelling visual communication with UAS. In: Hodicky, J. (ed.) MESAS 2016. LNCS, vol. 9991, pp. 81–98. Springer, Cham (2016). https://doi.org/10.1007/978-3-319-47605-6_7
6. Schelle, A., Stütz, P.: Visual communication with UAS: recognizing gestures from an airborne platform. In: Lackey, S., Chen, J. (eds.) VAMR 2017. LNCS, vol. 10280, pp. 173–184. Springer, Cham (2017). https://doi.org/10.1007/978-3-319-57987-0_14
7. Schelle, A., Stütz, P.: Gestural transmission of tasking information to an airborne uav. In: Yamamoto, S., Mori, H. (eds.) HIMI 2018. LNCS, vol. 10904, pp. 318–335. Springer, Cham (2018). https://doi.org/10.1007/978-3-319-92043-6_27
8. Cao, Z., Simon, T., Wei, S.-E., Sheikh, Y.: OpenPose: real-time multi-person keypoint detection library for body, face, and hands estimation. Carnegie Mellon University, Perceptual Computing Laboratory (2018). https://github.com/CMU-Perceptual-Computing-Lab/openpose
9. Kirk, D.: NVIDIA CUDA software and GPU parallel computing architecture. In: Proceedings of the 6th International Symposium on Memory Management, Montreal, Quebec, Canada, pp. 103–104. ACM, New York (2007). https://doi.org/10.1145/1296907.1296909
10. Yeo, H.-S., Lee, B.-G., Lim, H.: Hand tracking and gesture recognition system for human-computer interaction using low-cost hardware. Multimedia Tools Appl. (2015). https://doi.org/10.1007/s11042-013-1501-1
11. Schelle, A., Stütz, P.: Evaluierung eines symbolisch motivierten Gestenwortschatzes zur visuellen Kommandierung von unbemannten Flugsystemen (2019, manuscript submitted for publication)

Author Index

Printed in the United States
By Bookmasters